The Iron Scar

A Father and Son in Siberia

Trans-Siberian Railway

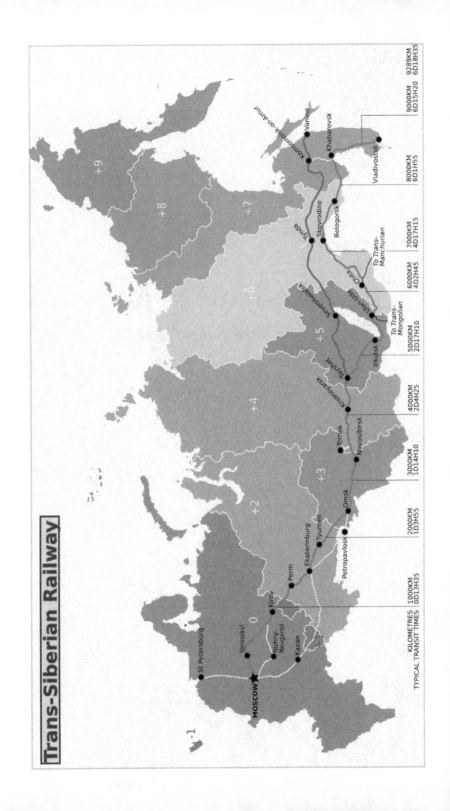

The Iron Scar

A Father and Son in Siberia

Bob Kunzinger

with photographs by
Michael Kunzinger

MADVILLE
PUBLISHING

Lake Dallas, Texas

FIRST EDITION

Requests for permission to reprint material from this work should
be sent to:

Permissions
Madville Publishing
P.O. Box 358
Lake Dallas, TX 75065

Author Photograph: Michael Kunzinger
Cover Design: Jacqueline Davis
Cover Art: "East of Irkutsk" by Michael Kunzinger

ISBN: 978-1-948692-86-1 paperback, 978-1-948692-87-8 ebook
Library of Congress Control Number: 2021941188

This book is dedicated to my father, Fred,

and my son, Michael

"I will try and set down honestly and plainly, hiding
nothing and highlighting nothing, the story
of those years. I will try to tell, quite simply, what it was like."

—Walter Ciszek, SJ, *With God in Russia*

"It is not flesh and blood, but the heart that makes
us fathers and sons"

—Friedrich Schiller

"If we wait for the moment when everything, absolutely everything, is ready, we shall never begin."

—Ivan Turgenev, *Fathers and Sons*

One

Tracks

The trans-Siberian railroad runs from the Baltic through Russia's western cities and villages, through the great dense and ancient forest, cuts across the steppe and the taiga, turns down along the Amur River, pushes its back up against China, and reaches out its falling fingers to find Vladivostok on the Sea of Japan. It spans the massive Russian empire, spans decades, czarist reigns, it spans the birth and death of the Soviet Union, lifetimes of laborers, the deaths of exiles; this stretch of rail cuts a path through politics, dynasties, families, through a multitude of ethnicities, through suffocating summers and bone-cold winters, Arctic winters, frozen winters so cold the mere mention of the trans-Siberian railway to westerners conjures up images of ice and barren fields of snow. This train moves aside whatever stands in the way; rock and soil, marble, a crisscross of countless fallen birches and pines. A myriad of engineering principles makes this train run across these iron rails through green landscapes. It rolls over pools of spent oil, of human waste, to carry passengers past the eastern edge of Russia's frayed European fabric into the silent mystique of Asia. These rails carried opportunity to the Siberian outposts, while transporting millions to gulags and prison camps. It brought soldiers to war and home again, bodies home again, Jews from their homes to eastern towns during the pogroms, tourists trying to reach Baikal, businessmen hoping to spend a few days away from the city; it brought the nineteenth century into the twentieth and the twentieth century into the twenty-first, the west to the east, and the hopes of millions into the vast indifference of the Russian frontier. These packed train cars have slid past vast apathetic fields for more than one hundred years, and they've carried the confessions of gulag guards, of Bolshevik evangelists, the wit and subversive criticism of dissident poets, the last hopes of a dying imperial family; these carriages have carted east those feared in Moscow, those freed in prison camps but forced to flee no further than the next station on a frozen frontier; these cars moved multitudes to the wasteland beyond the Urals hoping to populate the eastern perimeter of Russia, leaving them there to die from disease and deadly winters.

This train moves though our lives carrying stories of strangers, companions who help us blend in despite compromised communication skills, creates brothers who bond over chess and Baltika beer on some late night/early morning leg just above the Mongolian border.

This rail car carries this father and son into Siberia, the "frozen tundra" where it is said nothing grows, and exposure to the elements kills the strongest of men. We follow a long line of fathers and sons who battled the elements both external and within, with enemies and with each other, as they barreled across Russia into the wasteland to which politicians in St. Petersburg and Moscow sent their enemies, fearful of their power but more fearful of making them martyrs. We are not feeling sorry for ourselves, however. Unlike our predecessors we actually chose this course, paid for the passage, opted into finding out who and what is across this reach of the longest lay of tracks on the planet.

Every story set in Siberia portrays characters wearing parkas but still freezing their asses off. This was the image carried by

Cold-War era kids like me. Not today, not anymore. It is a clear summer afternoon here in St. Petersburg, and the temperature today is in the seventies. My son, Michael, and I wear short sleeve shirts and carry our bags to the edge of the platform with the sign which dictates this train is our ride to Yekaterinburg, the city which separates east from west, our first destination on this fabled journey. Right now it is in the mid-eighties in that city, and we both hope the cabins on board are air-conditioned. The porter takes our bags, and the passengers—men mostly, and some boys—board. They all hold their tickets and scout the numbers on the sides of the train carriages. One man asks if we need assistance, and now, only now, it is finally clear to me that we are really doing this; after years of thinking about it, months of planning, thousands of dollars in air travel and train tickets, and countless hours of research about where to go and where not to go, my son and I are about to train across the widest wilderness on the planet.

We chose second class, which means purchasing tickets for beds in a cabin built for four, bunk beds to each side of the entrance. Each bunk is about the size of a twin mattress, has storage, a light, and is tucked away quite comfortably, though the space down the middle of the cabin, about the width of the heavy, locking door, is narrow enough that two passengers sitting on their bunks with their feet on the floor cannot do so directly in front of each other or they will bang each other's knees. The cabins are generally full, so Michael and I always have two other passengers sharing the ride and sharing the table between the beds against the outside wall, which is made up mostly of a generously sized window. Travelers in second class are mostly businessmen heading to or from a job, families of four who already have the means to afford such luxury, and that rarest of specimen: the tourist. Us. For just a few rubles more, passengers can purchase meals, but few do. The brown bag provided has a bottle of water, a piece of chocolate, and a small container of rice with meat—or as my son noted, wood chips. Besides, there is plenty of food to be found without succumbing to their grab-bag concoction.

If we had wanted to travel first class, I would have paid twice as much so as not to have cabin mates, but then, of course, what is the point? The foundation of travel is people, local people who have unique customs and dialects, who share advice and laughter and, sometimes, tea, a bottle of wine, or vodka. Traveling on the Siberian railroad with cabin mates means learning to share, learning to trust, spilling communication skills like hand signs and silly drawings onto the table between us and pushing detente to its limits. Traveling six thousand miles together in a closet-sized cabin also means possible exposure of ourselves, our thoughts and ambitions, to each other; stepping into that shared space which for most fathers and sons can be avoided at home.

Passengers in third class ride in a separate car altogether, built more like a narrow barracks with a multitude of bunks pushed against each other in haphazard ways, and those passengers have little access to or money for the dining car, their bags and suitcases tucked under their heads for lack of storage as they head to their summer datchas. It is cheap, and it gets them where they need to go. When this two-continent-long ride was still in its infancy, there were only the extremes—Imperial travel with red velvet walls and inlay tables covered with the finest cuisine from the best chefs; or the cars filled with workers, exiles, going as far into the bleak distance as their health allowed. But today this train carries every conceivable aspect of Russian society, a veritable cultural cutout from some ethnography museum. And we are all wrapped by some steel casing brushing time aside as we click along, some for hours, some for days, some until someone else says it is time to disembark and start over. For all of its potential claustrophobic sorrow, this train is all about starting over.

The trans-Siberian railroad moves with bullet-like precision ripping holes through customs and cultures across nearly half the planet, with a history that pulled the 19th century expanse of Czarist Russia into the 20th century and the dominance of Soviet Russia, and then helped escort the mystique of so-called democratic Russia into the 21st century, all the while in its wake creating jobs, bringing people out of their ancient ways and setting a new course for anyone who hears its timeless and imposing rumble along this iron scar across Europe and Asia. The distance from St. Petersburg to Vladivostok is roughly six thousand miles, a journey of which very few travelers need or wish to engage. Perspective: it is as if I boarded the Long Island Railroad at Montauk Point to head to downtown Manhattan and decided to continue on well past Honolulu. We are an anomaly. The other travelers, nearly all men, are heading to or from work projects or visiting family just one or two stops away. Some people travel farther, but not more than a station or two, and in third class a few families carry a month's worth of belongings. As for the passengers going the distance, it seems to be just the two of us and a family of four from France, and we are all a little anxious. I have read all the books and watched the films, and I cannot think of a single positive image from history or even culture that conveys anything remotely cheerful or positive about this journey. Still, here we are.

When I was young, I rode trains with my father to midtown Manhattan. My siblings and parents and I trekked the couple of hours from eastern Long Island to "the city" to see a show and have dinner. It was like a magic trick, the way the rail carved its way through towns and past jammed highways and crowded streets, sweeping us right into the heart of New York. I was nervous, surrounded by strangers, skyscrapers, blaring car horns and blistering heat, but it was all so addicting, like we were the only explorers on the train and all the others were just props, extras. There is something nefariously narcotic about the exhilaration of unknown places. Now I'm fifty years older and somehow, I feel safer here on the Siberian rail. Maybe it is experience, or perhaps it is being well-prepared which calms my nerves and welcomes what is next. Most likely, it is simple resignation: we are here, we will board, and the train will leave the station. No magic tricks. And I know that small boy holding my father's hand is here as well, and my son when he was a child playing with his Brio Trains asking where we could go, him and I, in that yet unchanged and wondrous tone small boys have, he's here too, and my father riding the subway from Bay Ridge, Brooklyn, to Wall Street, just twenty-one, learning to navigate his way through it all; we're all on this journey which started a long time ago, half a century ago. More. A journey I like to think started before the trains, the tracks, the idea of steel and steam, when nothing but wilderness filled the spaces, a concept began in the quiet of that world absent of locomotion, when distance was measured in yards, not time zones.

We are far from the first father and son engaged by this railway. Czar Alexander the Third ordered his son Nicholai to start the project, and the young prince took it to heart, pouring his energy and ambitions into carving this legacy onto the Russian landscape. He hired a Scottish engineer and that man's son to figure it all out. The engineer brought in fellow countrymen and went to work under Nicholai's guidance, and the Scottish influence is still obvious all along the route. A few decades after his father's decree, that young prince became Czar Nicholas the Second, the so-called "Last Czar" of Russia, who in 1918 boarded the train with his son Alexi on this same route from St. Petersburg to Yekaterinburg for what would be the last ride of their lives. One hundred years ago that father and son, the boy's four sisters and their mother, Alexandra, rode to their new home in an old palace. These tracks beneath us now brought them to their fate. I stare down the line aware that this is that same rail, and we are heading to that same city, and will soon look out and see the same landscape seen by the Czar and his son, perhaps standing between the cars in the passageways, watching the small shacks and endless birch trees go by, not knowing what was next; that last time before the entire family was shot to death in the basement of their palace.

Michael and I come here to follow those Romanovs, to follow Chekhov, Tolstoy, Dostoevsky, the Bolsheviks, communists, tourists, laborers, dissidents, exiles, businessmen, to follow them seven time zones across one nation. To ride the railway from this first station to the last is to cross centuries, generations, and cultural differences so drastic some areas are not recognizable as sharing a common history. I glance at Michael who stares at maps and signs; I smile and remember the words of Czar Alexander in a letter to Nicholai, and I say, "Son, it is necessary to proceed at once for the *ride* on this line," and he nods, smiles, and stands up a bit straighter, as we begin the first leg. It was in that simple, hand-written note Alexander III wrote to his son that the idea of the crossing became reality. Nicholas, standing in Vladivostok waiting notice, opened the letter and read, "It is necessary to proceed at once to the construction of the line." Nicholas, understanding finally his fate, not yet knowing how fatalistic the railway would be to his yet-to-be-born family, placed a rock at what would become the eastern most point of the project. And us, here, on the other end, at the westernmost point of the TSRR, step on board.

We have come here, not driven as much as pulled, not so much to fulfill a dream as to fill a gap, to diagram the long and compound sentence which is the trans-Siberian railroad. Michael is on the edge of adulthood, me somewhere in the middle, both ready to see what is next, to move forward into something self-defining. Although the time of travel from start to finish is roughly a week, it will take us about three weeks with stops and wandering. Our first leg to Yekaterinburg takes about two days. We opted for this north route instead of the more common route from St. Petersburg to Moscow and then east.

"That's probably where all the tourists are," I say, knowing how most people follow that line into Siberia before heading south through Mongolia to China, ending in Beijing. But this journey of ours has little to do with tourism. I want to see what Russians have seen for a century. I will soon enough discover as we ride farther east that there is little difference now than there ever was in the books I have read, published nearly a century ago. This is a country whose politics remained fluid while the people and landscape did not. Heading from west to east, the motion of life slows down, the people too, growing more stagnant as the landscape grows sparse.

We have little idea of what to expect, no common ground upon which to even make a guess from any of our other travels, and both of us completely lack the language skills to navigate even the dinner menu. We are, in a sense, self-exiled pilgrims relying upon our faith in strangers; strangers who, for the majority of my life, I was taught not to trust and that they hated Americans. Yet, standing here now looking down the tracks beyond the dozen or so train cars, my soul settles down, finally able to reach beyond that terror which comes with anticipation, ignorance, and misinformation. And just by virtue of resignation to the fact there is no turning back, I find comfort in the kinetic reality of boarding, finding our cabin, seeing the sheets and pillows folded on our beds; and I know we both feel eased by the welcome bag filled with a bottle of water, chocolate, and tea, and the slow-growing sense of belonging. Here, now, seeing as far as I can down these tracks in the late afternoon of the White Nights, I cannot help but think of my own father standing on the platform of that Long Island station, waiting for the express to Manhattan, He made that journey every day for decades without complaint and with the same methodical purpose he would use to get dressed or fill the car with gas—a necessary, subconscious action. My dad, who is at the end of his rides, the end of this own journey, sat in the seats facing forward and read the paper, nodded to comrades continuing downtown with him, and in the afternoons on the way home he might break up the hour and a half trip with a drink in the bar car. That was his ride every day to and from Wall Street. And this is my son's and mine, individual trips for two men. I want to figure out what is next as a father whose son is moving on and as a son whose father is moving on as well. Naturally, being so far from home, the sense of some sort of oneness, of partnership, is strong between Michael and me. We will head east to the other side of the planet through the remote forests of Siberia, where I am told our closest traveling companions are whatever ghosts we bring along to talk to on the long hauls through endless nights. There is something about the absolute stillness of long-distance travel that makes time re-align itself and allows perspective to permeate those nights, allows us to excise our demons and watch them drift into our past as we trek along.

You cannot buy therapy like this in the states. There are too many towns, too much noise, and too much conversation. Everyone is always talking to someone. In America we already know how to get where we are going without a need to ask for help because we keep track; and even if we get lost, we can check our phones and get back on track. We keep track of where we have been, and if we are late, we hustle up and make tracks. We demand of ourselves to stay on track. We ride the rails to get home to our family and find comfort in some small tract of land. Oh, these Siberian rails run from the Imperial capital on the Baltic to the naval town on the Sea of Japan, to the land of exiles, of Decembrists, of Solzhenitsyn. They run so far into the wild, dark distance it is difficult to try and keep track.

The last time I rode a train my hopes and dreams were in their infancy, and now our passage is imminent, our bags are on board, and we are either destined or condemned to see this through. On previous trips to St. Petersburg, I walked by this station dozens of times in this cultural heart of Russia, Peter's City, but never gave it a glance. Now we are inside our own metaphor, boarding the train and seeing where it brings us, sometimes exploring, sometimes just enjoying the sound and the enchanting suggestion of forward motion. It is the way of things on this train across the earth, that at times we disembark to take a break, to explore another way; some companions will be with us longer than others, and some so briefly we will forget they were there to begin with; some of this ride will terrify us, some of it will excite us, and some of it will bore us to death, but still we ride. For some, a time will come when they wonder why they don't just step off for good, wish they never boarded to begin with, and some will continue on anyway but with resignation, some with determination, and some with no expectations at all.

That's us.

Two

Passages

Michael and I stand in the passage between cars and look at the landscape while he plays "This Land is Your Land" on the harmonica. Birch trees dominate the August distance, and for quite some time we pass little more than white tree trunks with green pastures and the occasional small shack alongside the tracks. Some shacks have guards who stand outside smoking cigarettes and watch us pass, but mostly the small guard houses remain empty, and all are painted either a pale yellow or a royal blue, all of them; as if someone in Moscow one summer day handed paint to some poor worker and said, "Go brighten up the place."

The striking reality of this "place" is that the landscape outside remains as much a part of the journey as the hallways inside, as much a companion as our cabin mates, and as essential to the crossing as the dining car and the thousands of miles of tracks still ahead. For the most part, the train itself is the tourist attraction here; it is hotel, dining car, and late-night pub. In America, we train through somewhere else on our way to where we are going, but in Russia, the somewhere else *is* our traveling companion, the arc of our narrative, the string of dynamic moments in our character development. Tolstoy points out, "One of the first conditions of happiness is that the link between man and nature shall not be broken." This is true as well on a train; especially so, since it is the "trans-Siberian" part of this journey that makes the ride unique. We are not out here for a train ride; we are here for the "trans-Siberian" train ride. This land is not like passing through the Adirondacks, no matter how similar the surroundings may sometimes seem. This terrain remains, for all intents and purposes, mostly barren of towns and people, making the train a moving oasis, and it is exactly that contrast which provides balance and makes anyone on this ride aware of each nuance of the journey, and it is that vague "barrenness" which keeps us from forgetting exactly where we are. Certainly, closer to the city when we first left St. Petersburg, the surroundings seemed more suburban than either city or rural, but once we pass Lake Ladoga just a few hours later, any semblance of towns slips into the shadows and we quickly discover this train remains the most essential element. In most of the stretches of this ride, the population on board is indeed significantly higher than the residents in the surrounding territory.

"'Slow Train' by Dylan," I say, and Michael smiles. He knows the tune, and he knows if he cannot retort within a minute, he buys the next round in the dining car. I throw it out there while he plays "This Land is Your Land," figuring it difficult to call up a different tune so quickly while playing another and a third on his mind. It is one of our games; this one "train songs." He continues to play for half a minute, then says, "Midnight Train to Georgia," and returns to Guthrie without missing a beat. "The other Georgia," he adds, and I laugh.

The narrow hallways in the carriages are often crowded with Russians looking out the windows which run along the length of the corridor. None of it is overly confining or claustrophobic, but on a week-long journey across wilderness, sharing a cabin with businessmen whose dialect is hardly recognizable as Russian, we find respite here between cars where we can hear the rails beneath us and feel some coolness coming in the moving floor.

These carriage connections are something akin to tectonic plates sliding back and forth so when we stand against the walls facing each other one of us might be moving in the opposite direction of the other, but not too much and it is all so much smoother than we had expected, and some passengers passing through to the dining car might pause for a moment, look out the windows and listen to Michael play American folk music. It is odd to feel at home in a land so far from our own, and the farther east we move toward an absence of western Russian architecture or cars or really any sense of village life at all except guards near small yellow and royal-blue shacks, the easier it is to believe we are moving across the upper mid-west in America, or across Canada where such vast wilderness might still be possible.

The first stretch of this trip is not unlike the ride through Nassau County on the way from Manhattan to the emptier farmland of eastern Long Island. This stretch out of the city of Peter the Great has the same sprawl of factories and endless roads, empty lots, elementary schools not improved in forty years, stores, rows of parked cars along narrow streets, scattered trees, tiny stores with small windows beneath Cyrillic words, random garages, industrial sites ad nauseum, and the shacks. The train makes more frequent stops now than it will tomorrow and the stations here are more crowded with men in suits and women in heels and children carrying hard suitcases filled with clothes and toys.

In the city, changes can be so immediate and drastic, it is numbing. One day it is Leningrad; the next St. Petersburg; one day the markets use the traditional ways of shopping— pick out your goods from behind the counter, go to a different line to pay, return to the first line to turn over your receipt for the goods—and the next day you're putting all your goods from the shelves into a cart then onto a conveyor belt where someone bags it all and you walk out like you just left a western superstore. No transition, no warning, no sense of what-was in the sudden world of what-is. Ironically, in the villages far from the city, changes can be as drastic yet paradoxically irrelevant. The owners of the local businesses and factories have changed so now money ends up in the pockets of some oligarchs in Moscow instead of the government in Moscow—but what do local workers care? People still work at the same garage they always have, the same factory, the local store. Maybe more customers from the city show up, but otherwise life is the same since no one in these small hamlets had any knowledge of, or any need to know, where the profits went to begin with. They live their lives, and once in a while they ride this train east, to visit family or find work. Life in the city and in the rural spread of Russia is similar for that disconnected routine.

Farther east, the city-sprawl eventually gives way to villages with their own center, disconnected from St Petersburg in the daily ways of life, with their own soul of sorts, a town square, an abandoned or repurposed estate, and some notable industry. These are the villages which mark time as we know it. In these towns-as-we-think-of-them, people try and balance the changes with home improvements such as satellite dishes, new appliances, and foreign-made cars, all tempered by traditional garden plots tended with archaic tools. Throughout the run along the rails out of St Petersburg nearly all the way to Yekaterinburg, small gardens back each another with tiny sheds for supplies. This is shared land, and everyone learned generations ago to respect each-other's plots, their vegetables, their place in time. And the farther we travel the sparser the space between villages, and I am overwhelmed by the seeming distance from what in the west might be defined as "civilization." It tempers my nervous bend, and I am reminded of Tolstoy's words, "I felt a wish that my present frame of mind might never change."

In these regions, the railroad stations become the focus of the lives of locals. The train is their commerce, and we are their customers, their connection to the rest of the world, their topic of conversation and their method for keeping track of time. We all have our own reasons to travel through Siberia, and each of the stations of the crossing has its purpose beyond the simple ritual of passengers boarding and disembarking. It is mail depot, food court for old women selling homemade goods, gathering spot for children home from school, and they all bear it well, conduct their business well.

Marshes sometimes appear, or fields of grass and hay, and wheat, and runs of grazing land with scattered cattle seemingly without guidance. A shack appears, and wires run along the rail. Every hour or so a few roads converge around a few houses, and a car rolls to a stop next to the tracks, and I wonder where it is going. It cannot be east, I foolishly believe, since it seems to me there isn't anything in the east except that mysterious and vast nothingness which awaits us through the great northern forest. I will soon discover I am wrong, but the vastness I see outside the windows in these passages becomes even more barren as we move closer to the eastern edge of "European Russia," so much so, in fact, that eventually the only visible life is our own reflection in the windows at dusk and the fading light on the tops of birch trees. At some point all landscapes require imagination to cover the darkening distances, landscape which is only barely visible during daylight to begin with, let alone when dusk fades; add to this mystique the curiosity on the part of middle-aged westerners like me about the outposts of Siberia, the villages in the east, the fabled prisons, the isolation and cold. It is not difficult to understand how the railway needs this wilderness, these villages, in order that it successfully cross the breadth of the country. But the iron rails have become elemental in the lives and livelihood of everyone who lives within earshot of the rumbling carriages.

For now I turn my attention to a passing Russian man who nods with a smile as he moves toward the dining car. The sun has set, so studying the wilderness of this expansive nation will have to wait for another day as it is finally, and completely, dark. Those villages outside, however, seem to be mirrored on board in the hallways and sleeping quarters, each cabin a cottage, each passenger a resident, safe inside this artery running through Europe into Asia. The balance of inside and out, of engineering and wilderness, simply means we are as much a part of what we pass at fifty miles-an-hour as we are a part of conversations in the dining car. It may be the twenty-first century in the cabins, but something older and weathered waits in the lands stretching across the Urals and the Steppe. They lay out as dioramas of decades in decline, a wilderness witness to slaughters, pogroms, transports, exiles, and dissidents, and this train has been an accomplice in this tragic history. During the day the brilliant, warm sun on the landscape is inviting, primal, but as night falls, the shadows blend history and place, so that out among the faded trees it seems as if ghosts gather and wave as we ride past. *This land wasn't made for czars*, I think, *let alone presidents or general secretaries*. It is the most untamed place I have ever been, though I haven't really been "to" what we have come to call "out there" as much as we are passing through. Another great irony of the journey is for most of the crossing, we never really are in Siberia; we are in a train looking at Siberia. Still, anyone on board can easily witness the beautiful, ancient, and timeless sameness about it, its horror and tragedy, its heroism and redemption, and standing here now it is easier to believe that those historic and not so long-ago terrors along the rails were merely fleeting moments which never could take hold with any permanence. Nature wins, as always, and out on this majestic stretch of rail, where Europe lies with its spine against the awakening Asian continent, Michael's resounding harp-playing snaps me back on board.

Standing between cars is only slightly louder than inside any individual train car because despite being "sort of" outside, these spaces between—the gangway connections as they are called—

are designed nothing like the locomotives in television westerns where cowboys leap after each other across iron joints and passing tracks. These are mostly enclosed passages, pleasantly cooler than the hot cabins but decidedly not exposed to the elements. Every alternating passage between cars is reserved for smokers, and since so many Russians smoke while traveling by train, those passages are normally filled. Michael and I stand by ourselves between the cars in the odd, non-smoking passages, and he plays Guthrie while I look out at the wilderness with dusk coming on, out at the same land Angela Carter describes in *Night at the Circus* as the caravan crosses into Asia: "Outside the window, there slides past that unimaginable and deserted vastness where night is coming on, the sun declining in ghastly blood-streaked splendor like a public execution across, it would seem, half a continent, where live only bears and shooting stars and the wolves who lap congealing ice from water that holds within it the entire sky. All white with snow as if under dustsheets, as if laid away eternally as soon as brought back from the shop, never to be used or touched. Horrors! And, as on a cyclorama, this unnatural spectacle rolls past at twenty-odd miles an hour in a tidy frame of lace curtains only a little the worse for soot and drapes of a heavy velvet of dark, dusty blue."

Our train chugs along thirty-miles-an hour faster than Carter's, and the timeless and borderless tone of the harmonica brings me back to the moment at hand, and it is a scene out of Guthrie's own life, a page of *Bound for Glory*, and I think how every young man should experience this freedom, this absolute sense of the moment. Here, Michael has his first taste of the wild possibilities before him in the middle of what was once one of the most restrictive empires and then one of the most invasive governments in the history of humanity. I watch him play while he watches the dark outline of trees rip by, and I take note of how good he has become. The disappearing sun lay flat behind me, catching a glint on his harp, and he looks older, like he belongs, like I am but another Russian passing between cars, and he is simply here, and it makes sense, and I listen to him somehow keep Guthrie's repetitive melody from being boring. He nods toward a blue shack with a solitary guard illuminated by a solitary lamp on a post nearby, and keeps playing, a talent he apparently managed to master while I was passing through his youth on my way to work. *It turns out we have been riding this train for twenty years*, I think, and so far, it seems to me, we have managed to stay on track. So while I desire to experience all aspects of our pilgrimage, from meeting passengers in third class to conversing with the dining car attendants, I cannot help but admit how much more I value our moments in the gangway connections, the music, and our quiet conversations. He is carrying his cameras and I have my journals, separate arts, different means of communication, his more immediate and spontaneous, mine more reflective, but in our individual ways we come together here, in the passage, in the arts, in this larger place we will forever remember as "our Siberian journey."

Michael dips his harmonica. "'Take the 'A' Train' by Ellington," he says, familiar with the tune I whistled for years. He plays louder to make a reply more difficult to conceive, and he is right. Tonight's round is on me, even though I quickly recall a half-dozen compositions. *Downtown Train, Crazy Train, Casey Jones*, and that Springsteen one which escapes me at the moment. There is something about the train motif which all artists have borrowed and shared to satisfy our common metaphor. "'Everyone loves the Sound of a Train in the Distance,' Paul Simon," I say, but he shakes his head. It is too late. We laugh.

These times we spend together in this passage have become our small shared American space. When we enter our cabin or the dining car or stand in the hallway looking out the wall-size windows at the landscape, conversation inevitably occurs with other passengers and then we are separate, he and I, two

American travelers who happen to be father and son barreling through a foreign land. But in this passageway, quiet, we find something familiar. It is normal to need some place like this when traveling—a pub, a church, a coffee shop—a place to find one's bearings and catch one's breath. It does not need to be for long, the length of a tune, perhaps.

Another passenger stops to note we are Americans and that we are father and son. He smiles and says how wonderful. "Otleechna!" Excellent! It doesn't escape me that many fathers and sons do not have this chance; and I am certain Michael is aware as well. If he wasn't before this trip, every person we meet tells us so: "Oh how special it is to be able to travel across Russia together. You'll remember this forever!" We always respond as if no one has reminded us of this before. The truth is, I never tire of hearing it.

Michael stops playing to take a photograph of mysterious fields of cattle with no apparent farmhouse or farmer, but the light is gone, and he gives up. I wonder what happened in some man's ancestry or some parental political bend that finds him on a farm in the middle of nowhere to tend cattle without neighbors, without news, without much interaction with other men. Then Michael plays again and the music brings me back inside where I watch him lean against the wall of the car, hands cupped around the edges of his harmonica, a thousand miles of track behind us, and I laugh out loud at the convergence of circumstances that finds me with my twenty-year-old son on a train rolling across the former Soviet Union toward the Pacific, the vague destination of Vladivostok, just a dot on a map, closer to Hawaii than to where we are now, with no apparent purpose other than to enjoy the ride, playing and singing American folk songs. It did not take long for us to settle into our own lives in our own cabin, feeling like this land was made for him and me.

Three

Moscow Time

Before we left Virginia, my father asked if we were ready for the trip and if I were as certain as I could be that everything would be fine. "We're all set!" I told him, sorry he could no longer travel, sorry he could no longer clearly see any pictures I might show him. "Dad!" I said, "What could possibly go wrong?!" and we all laughed.

Here's what went wrong:

Tickets to ride the trans-Siberian railroad the way we are run roughly $1000 dollars each in second class. That does not include transfers, flights, food, hotels—well, everything else. A friend in Russia whom I trust and who knows the Russian travel business told me the most efficient and dependable agency for Americans to book tickets for the rail is "Real Russia," based in London. I arranged for the tickets, filling out a simple form online to let them know where and when I wanted to get off the train all along the route, and for how long. I then let a friend of mine who is a tour operator in Russia know I would need hotel reservations in those cities and the arrival and departure dates based upon the train schedule. It was all very easy, and I was able to complete most of the arrangements in less than an hour with some online, user-friendly forms which, thank God, would not let me book the wrong times. Still, the price increased with every button I pushed, and each time I booked something new, a prompt reminded me the cost was completely non-refundable, and if we should ever miss a train connection anywhere along the route, we are out of luck—we have to start over—we must buy new tickets—if seats are even still available. This warning was clear. I kept waiting for the last prompt to read, "If you change your mind or miss a connection, you're screwed," but it did not. Close though.

I also bought three meals for the duration of each leg of the journey, and when we were on board, someone asked what meal we wanted. It was not much extra, which was good since the provided food sucked. But the dining car was not expensive, and the food was excellent. Also, no one told us until we were at the first stop out of St. Petersburg that old women at the stations come from the local villages and sell food—berries, perogies, dried fish, hot pockets filled with onions and potatoes, and pastries. These homemade delicacies are delicious and inexpensive. Moreover, they bring us as close as one can get to village life and traditions without actually walking from the station into the neighborhood.

My point is this: the cost adds up. Fast. But we were booked, and the London agency sent a letter with all the details, including our itinerary down to the exact minute, as well as hard copies of the actual train tickets for the entirety of the journey. The agency in Russia sent me hotel confirmations and arranged for transport from the stations to our hotels all along the route, and I used all of those confirmations to secure a Russian Visa—each another few hundred dollars. We could not secure the visas without proof of places to stay and departure tickets.

We were ready. I had a list of everything we would need to know in chronological order: Flight times, passports and visas, ground transportation, hotel stay in Russia the first few nights simply to adjust before boarding, the train schedule, confirmations for hotels in other cities, tickets for return flights, batteries, charger, journal, cash—a lot of cash in small bills since

ATM's simply have not yet reached the train stations of Siberia and credit cards are worthless on board.

In Yekaterinburg, the train depot is a stone's throw from a motel. It is a wide street with four lanes of cars, and to assist in crossing there is a walking tunnel beneath the road, leaving the impression the city is busy and uninteresting. But that is simply not true. We explored for a full two days this fourth largest city in Russia on the western edge of Asia, named after Peter the Great's wife, Catherine the First. The city is a mixture of new and old Russia. There are western cafés, concerts, and clothing stores, but there are also remnants of the old Soviet methods, like standing in line at a grocer, trucks selling containers of sour cream, and guards with guns in the hotel, something I have not seen since the early '90's in St. Petersburg just after the coup. Still, local students prepared a grunge music festival and gaming booths line the boardwalk along the river. A woman sells city souvenirs from a cart behind the Church on Blood, and another vendor sells ears of corn next to a row of ice cream carts. The waterfront of Yekaterinburg is not unlike any in Europe with outdoor cafes and young servers making money before heading back to college. Except for the Cyrillic signs, this could be Amsterdam or Rome. We find bakeries on many corners, a beautiful photography museum with a host who gives Michael a stack of photography books when she learns that is his profession, and a man standing next to a 19th century wooden building invites us in to see the weapons used during the final stretch of the Czarist regime.

But in Yekaterinburg for all of its modern improvements, the culture of rural Russia is just a few kilometers away, and the city does not let you forget you're leaving Europe, both figuratively and literally. What lies ahead is the grandest stretch of forest in the world, with barely a population to account for, and a torrid history of exiles, gulags, and native populations dating back thousands of years. Just on the other side of the

European/Asian line lay the descendants and stories of Tartars, Mongols, and more. It is hard not to think of our journey as one back in time as well as ahead on the world clock. Like any rural place in America, the advances in life come more slowly as the distance grows from the city center, and time sometimes is not measured in days and years, but centuries and empires.

There is a strong melancholic presence for Czarist Russia in this city, and this sentiment is most notably obvious at the church built on the site where Nicholas the Second and his family were slaughtered in the middle of the night. The "Church on Blood" here in Yekaterinburg, the full name of which is "The Church on Blood in honor of All Saints Resplendent in the Russian Land," is one of two similarly named cathedrals in this vast nation. Alexander the Second was assassinated in St. Petersburg and the Cathedral of the Spilled Blood rose where he was killed. And this one, built on the spot where his grandson, Czar Nicholas and his family, met their fate.

The Czar and his family boarded their Imperial train on this track and rode in style to the palace here in the Urals. What a train ride that must have been. Did they know it was most likely their last? Did young Alexi, whose two heroes were his father and the Siberian priest, Rasputin, know his fate would follow that of his friend, the "Healing Priest"? Did he sense he would be shot next to his four sisters in the basement of that palace? Did Nicholas and Alexandra still hold out hope they could regain the throne, or did they discuss how they would now live in exile, a life perhaps in Paris with other relatives who had already fled? Instead, they died at the hands of the Bolsheviks, their remains buried in the mountains and not discovered until the 1990's, just about twenty years before our trip, and all seven were eventually reinterned at St Peter and Paul Cathedral inside the walls of the fortress in St. Petersburg, in a small room in the church which holds the sarcophagi of his predecessors back to Peter the Great. I was there that day in the

'90s when they opened the small chapel for the first time, and we all stood together as a guide spoke of their ride east, their descent into the basement, their demise, and their discarded bodies lost for another seventy-five years. I did not know that my then toddler son and I would stand on the grounds of that palace in Yekaterinburg less than twenty years later. In Russia, history is always present, blurring the lines of the present and making whatever might happen next seem tethered to whatever happened before.

After that 1918 massacre, the Yekaterinburg Palace was left in disrepair, then destroyed, and in its stead rose the "Church on Blood"; today, the basement where they were killed is a shrine. Michael and I stand quietly and light candles, noting the myriad images, icons, photographs, and engravings to the family. He buys me a small wooden plaque with a photograph of Czar Nicholas II and his son Alexi, looking very much like a father and son who love each other and enjoy whatever time they can spare together. That is my father and me, drinking Scotch and watching baseball; it is my son and me, exposing our souls out on the edge of western culture, and this is Russia—a country it seems whose every next step is determined by her past, one which reaches out but with hesitant hands, and allows the future to unfold all the while it whispers, "You are taking your past with you, always." This country's DNA is always present tense, no matter what era is being examined. I think about the family's shock at that first sign of guns, their screams, the silence after, the smell of smoke, their blank, dead stares, all if it right here, under our feet, just yards away. I think of my father, born just seven years after that slaughter, of my son, and of the deception of linear time. Standing here now, I'm not so certain time doesn't somehow circle back on itself, making sure we don't neglect what was.

The hotel in Yekaterinburg, too, is a clash of cultures, both Soviet and post-coup Russia, with even some small, excruciatingly slow Stalin-era elevators. It, too, reminds me of St Petersburg back in the early nineties when Oligarchs bought up everything they could and gave jobs to anyone loyal to them, even if that meant too many men wandering around large lobbies, some with guns, while outside a few chauffeurs wait to give someone a ride across town. As the years went by and the people of this country got their collective act together, the Soviet habits faded from view, if not from practice. Wandering around most of this city is not unlike being in Paris or Amsterdam with canals and cafes, until we return to the lobby of the hotel.

We have enjoyed our time in this city, and we agree it has the feel of an American college town—young and alive and untethered by tradition despite the persistent presence of its tragic history. Still, in just a few hours we need to head to the station for the second leg of our lengthy sojourn, the one which will bring us decidedly into Siberia. We had been planning this trip for a year, and I had been dreaming of this—crossing the Russian Empire from the Baltic to the Sea of Japan—for a decade, and here we are, shedding the familiarity of Europe for the mystery of the east. I always assumed the only people who would make this journey did so by force, exiled by Czars and General Secretaries, to finish out their life in a labor camp, or for the lucky ones, start a new life in a village to do as they wish, far from having any influence over the easily swayed mobs of Moscow and St Petersburg.

But even a hundred years ago some made this journey by choice. What courage that would take back then. It wouldn't be much different than my grandfather's grandfather, who with his brothers left Germany so long ago that communication was cut off for a minimum of months at a time. There was no device with which to keep in contact. They were simply gone. But they were hopeful, looking for a new place to be from. Their decision to set sail and not return was a self-imposed exile, and my son is the youngest result, the current reason for their exodus, the latest in the line of forward motion.

And like my ancestors who arrived in America, I am now in a land where I don't speak the language, I don't know anyone, I have no translators, and most of the travelers are drinking. This isn't wholly unusual when one travels often, but I must admit a slight rise in anxiety in these conditions occurring in one of the few regions of the world still mostly barren of anything other than strictly local customs, people, and expectations. With this, we enter Asian-Russia. As we said from the start: "Well, it will be an adventure." This is my father's fault. He instilled in me a sense of exploration when he bought me books by or about Robert Louis Stevenson, Woody Guthrie, Robin Lee Graham, and even Anton Chekhov. It is likely that what we read as children will be the dictate of our trajectory. But I wonder now if those souls in those pages sought out faraway places because of the books their fathers bought them? Probably. With my son, however, we jumped quickly from the book-giving stage to the train depot. Where my father might have said "get a blanket and I'll read you a book," I turn to my son and say, "Grab your things and let's go." I'm sure this isn't new, and from the pilgrimages of pre-Christian explorers to the work projects of nineteenth century Scottish engineers, all of us keep working our way down the line.

On the first leg we had a cabin with two other travelers who kept leaving to visit friends in the next cabin. I guessed them to be a crew of construction workers heading to a job, mostly by their boots and clothes, but I had no idea. They were friendly enough, and when Michael set up his laptop and put on *Butch Cassidy and the Sundance Kid*, they stretched out in their bunks and watched, completely absorbed. In the hall a few men talked and laughed, and when one of us left to get tea or use the john, they remained quiet, would whisper something, laugh again, and then continue their conversation. It can be intimidating, but for some odd reason I have convinced myself our traveling companions throughout the journey might be merely curious, not knowing if I am a spy, psychotic, or possibly as drunk as them; perhaps all three. My twentieth century childhood, however, rarely allows that they figure us to be two tourists on a train. For now, I let them believe whatever they want; later, when my head re-cultures itself, I'll attempt communication. Since tourists generally don't travel this line, it's no surprise we attract attention. Still, it was relaxing when that leg was behind us and we settled into town and explored this historic Yekaterinburg.

Now, we are killing time at the hotel before heading to the station to board. My son writes in his journal and I gather some papers and finish what is left of a Baltika Beer. We are about to venture into "real" Russia, eastern Russia, Asian-continent Russia, vast forested Siberia; that wilderness on the other side of the Ural Mountains which stretches thousands and thousands of miles to the Pacific. As we head east, to the north is barren or forested nothingness; to the south a slew of railroad-inspired villages where the stations are the center of activity. There are a few other major cities along the way such as Novosibirsk, Omsk, Ulan-Ude, and, of course, Irkutsk, our next stop several days from now, but we can already sense that the further east we travel on the trans-Siberian Railway, the more time is out of joint.

We sit in the hotel room and gather our energy to walk across the thoroughfare to the station. Our train is scheduled to leave at eight p.m., so we lounge around, read, relax, and talk about how much we look forward to Irkutsk. We talk about what we have seen the last two days, including the heart-wrenching museum and cathedral. We are tired and sunburnt from the eighty-degree temperatures and the bright day. Michael writes, and I glance at the tickets in some sort of compulsive need to know again that 20 hundred hours is 8 o'clock, just over two hours away since it is just 6 p.m..

Then I read the ticket.

The train is to depart at 1806, six minutes after six, six

minutes away; about the time it takes just to catch the ancient, tiny elevator to the lobby. My heart sinks. I yell for Michael to grab his things; I grab mine, bypassing my normal compulsive inspection of the hotel room to make sure we don't leave anything behind. He asks if I am misreading what at home we call military time, but I am not. We ride the elevator and I read on the agent's sheet that she did, in fact, write 2006, but the actual, official, paid in full, use it or you are screwed ticket says 1806 and at this moment I'm trusting the tickets more than the lady in London who wrote this cover letter.

We run, negotiating the traffic on the highway rather than take the extra valuable minutes by going through the tunnels. At fifteen minutes past six we arrive at the station, nine minutes after the train's scheduled departure time according to the ticket. I struggle with the Russian language on the board, look for the next stop on our journey, but it is not listed. I ask everyone in front of the terminal schedule, but every person politely shrugs and walks away. I eventually find a guard and ask about the train and he too shrugs, his hands up in an internationally recognizable apologetic manner: Sorry, he says, "Izveneetia; there is no train."

This is insane. I'm on the other side of the fucking world with my son, I don't speak the language enough to do more than order food and ask how to get to the train station, and we are stranded in a place where credit cards are worthless and tickets are expensive. It is getting late, and even if I manage to put together enough money to continue, there is no guarantee seats are available anyway.

I looked back at the hotel as if I could move back time. *What was I thinking by taking this ludicrous trip without any credentials?* I asked the random pillars of the entrance to the station. Michael stood reading the departure board hoping we missed "Irkutsk," and people around found new places to wait, a few feet further away from the crazy American cursing at some random clerk in England.

There are moments we remember all our lives; this is one

of them, those brief extremes in life—births, deaths, falling in love, being stranded in Siberia with no idea what to do next. I have long believed how we handle the situation has more effect on the outcome than the situation itself; if that was not true, all of us would have the same story at the end of the day, and worse, life would become predictable and monotonous. One thing has always been true about my life—it has never been either predictable *or* monotonous. Still, when I am standing on a platform with a feeling of complete helplessness, and my son is waiting for a clue as to what happens next, what happens next is what we will remember.

For a long time, people whose opinion I value had questioned my plans. One friend asked, "Siberia? What did you do? Are they making you go?" With few exceptions, this journey appeared to others as not well thought out, and to a certain degree that is true. But even with the best laid plans, being stranded is a random act. But within less than a minute with blood pressure rising and my stomach in sudden distress, my mind moved through all five stages of grief, and when I arrived at acceptance, some semblance of philosophy took hold and I thought, *Aren't I already stranded? Isn't that why I'm here—because life was stationary, the days were motionless, and I could see too far down the proverbial tracks?* My father, who I no longer blame for instilling this sense of adventure in me deciding instead that is paternal intuition recognized my restlessness, asked me one night during a commercial of a baseball game, "So what made you want to go to Siberia?"

My answer remains complicated. It was years ago. I attended a party in Virginia with writer Bob Shacochis, who in his book *Kingdoms in the Air,* records his travels on the Kamchatka Peninsula in northeast Siberia. Bob learned I had spent some time in St. Petersburg, Russia, and told me of his adventures on the other side of the nation, including a drinking tale of an incredibly rare but marvelous Siberian liquor which has been around since the fourteen hundreds. It is made from the soaked antlers of Maral deer, thought to make men strong in "many ways." I laughed hard and told him I would be right back. I went home and grabbed *my* bottle of Maral deer liquor which had been given to me as a gift the first time I taught in St. Petersburg, and I returned to the party where Bob and I retreated to the kitchen.

We bonded.

Before our eyes glazed over, he told me I had to see Siberia. It did not have to be Kamchatka, he insisted, but I simply must see the most remote and least understood wilderness in the world. It is timeless, he told me, and electric. It will make you miss home, he said, but you will never want to leave. "You're an American!" he exclaimed, pouring the last shot from the liter bottle shaped like a bear. "People will stare at you and talk about you everywhere you go, because anytime an American goes to Siberia it's considered an invasion," he added and laughed. And then a bit more serious, in a whisper, he said, "Besides, Bob. No one writes about Siberia anymore. They just don't."

I had wanted to travel to Siberia since I was a young journalism student with a desire to be John Reed and write my own *Ten Days that Shook the World*. I read about the trans-Siberian railway, about its penetration deep into the North Asian forests, about its use during the World Wars, and its use for the spread of propaganda during the Russian Civil War. I read its role as a character in Boris Pasternak's *Doctor Zhivago* as well as in various volumes by Solzhenitsyn, and my mind drifted toward the mystique and excitement of what might be the last great train adventure, certainly the longest, in the world.

Michael was ten at the time of the party, and for the next decade I stayed on track as a father, a college professor, and a sideline traveler reading all I could about the place, which was not much. It did not take long to discover Bob's comment about the lack of literature of the region was on the money— no one writes about Siberia anymore, and certainly not the railroad. I could find only one guidebook—one—by Bryn Thomas, though more would emerge after our journey; one picture book which portrays the trite image of a dark, frozen place since the travelers recorded their journey in winter, and one video of a couple from the United States who had hired guides and translators, turning their adventure into something closer to Disney than anything authentic.

Still, during those ten years the idea recessed as life rolled along. Sometimes I would hear the distant call of a train or buy a book or two about Russia, about the people, which my son read before I even had the chance, but an adventure like that was not in the cards for a young father. As a visiting professor and director of study abroad programs, I made a few dozen trips to St. Petersburg, once even taking the midnight train to Moscow, further igniting hopes of heading east. Through his teens Michael would tell me about the history of Siberia, and then about the landscape. It turns out there were, in fact, more books about Siberia than I or Shacochis thought. Michael picked up the Siberian trilogy by Colin Thubron, Ian Frazier's *Travels in Siberia*, and more. He would read passages of Bruce Lincoln's *The Conquest of a Continent*, which exposes some of the most incomprehensible cruelty of invasion, and Anna Reid's *The Shaman's Coat*, which engaged me for her journalistic approach to introducing the most endearing and seemingly friendly indigenous people. We read Benson Bobrick's *East of the Sun*, which might be the most valuable for exposing the history and social climate of the region, and, of course, Dervla Murphy's *Through Siberia by Accident*, which describes "one of the bleakest, most inhospitable" regions of the world. I was not satisfied with that interpretation, however. Of course, these works somehow demystified Siberia while at the same time redeveloped my intrigue. But they all lacked what I sought and, in turn, supported Bob's insistence on that lack of writing: there was work about "Siberia," just not any addressing the adventures of being on the train, crossing this nearly immeasurable wilderness, and meeting the people in the passage, the crew, the stationmasters along the way. Few people wrote much about *that*, and when they did, they remained in some literal, travelogue approach. Their prose lacked the necessary significance to keep me engaged. At the time of our departure, David Green's on-point and finely written *Midnight in Siberia: A Train Journey into the Heart of Russia*, had not been released. The only way I was going to read about a train on the far side of the world, I decided, is if it was as much about me as it was the landscape; I might only be able to relate to such an adventure if I was already a character on board.

That is when I learned about the actual construction of the rail. It is a story of an empire on its last legs, about the technological advances sweeping the world, and the desire to connect both east and west, future and past. We read about Czar Alexander III's decree which instilled in his son a sense of purpose; we read how that confidence helped the prince's rise to Czar and his determination to see the mission through and of another father and son team, engineers from Russia, the Cherepanovs, who adopted some British plans and developed the first steam engine and sent it to St. Petersburg.

And the significance of my own journey clarified itself: the tale of the trans-Siberian railroad is the story of fathers and sons. It is one of adventure and pain, discovery and abandonment, and I slowly understood that Shacochis had been right: I had to go to Siberia, but I added an element to my narrative: I had to bring Michael.

And now discovery has been overtaken by that sense of abandonment as we remain stranded in Yekaterinburg, and Michael stands on the train platform watching the blood run from his father's face. He waits to one side with our baggage deciphering the Cyrillic on the signs, still in the denial stage though I am afraid his Anger part is coming fast and just might be directed at me, and rightfully so I suppose. My stomach churns as I anticipate being out of luck on the literal edge of Siberia with not nearly enough money for even one of us to continue. Then a gentleman nearby says, "You are early. It leaves at 8:06, 20:06. At train station, all tickets marked in Moscow time; that is two hours before us."

I stare at the man. "Moscow time? Not local time?"

"No, all tickets throughout Russia on rail are registered in Moscow time. You can rest."

"That... is... confusing. Moscow time? Right now it is 6."

"No it is 4."

"But..."

"In Moscow it is 4, so here in station it is 4. If you go back outside, it is 6. That is why you are confused. You didn't notice when you took train here?"

"No, the ticket said we were leaving at five and we left at five."

"Oh, yes, that is because you were on Moscow time both inside and outside when you left. When you get to Vladivostok, it is seven hours ahead of Moscow time outside station in city, but inside station it is Moscow time. So right now in Vladivostok it is just after 11 p.m., but inside station it is 4 p.m.."

"That's dumb."

"Welcome to Russia."

Eventually, we board and find our new quarters. For the first part of this leg of the journey we share a cabin with two young, Russian businessmen. They are either finishing work in St. Petersburg and headed home, or they live in the city and are on their way to a job. These two do not even know it is English we speak; they think we speak Spanish. When we tell them it is English, they assume we are from England, and I let them for now. If I can break through to deeper conversation with anyone perhaps then I will give them more details of where we are from and where we are going.

I imagine our young Russian cabin mates are as apprehensive as us, wondering, "Who are these two Spaniards?" At least Michael and I have each other to talk to, but that is simply not good enough and derails one of the prime goals of this journey, and so we are both determined to cross that linguistic gap and get to know these traveling companions. Being out here alone would be the true adventure, but I was not raised that way. Safety first. Funny how many times I ignored that rule. Now here I am hoping Michael wanders away, meets people and manages conversation. He will play his harmonica; people will listen. He will bring his chess set to the dining car and people will want to play. Music and chess are universal. Communication is easy; language is a different story.

When the train finally leaves, I turn off all devices with a clock. My life at home is ruled by time, by schedules, so by God I will take advantage of this crossing into Asia, seemingly into some other century. And soon we will be staring out the window toward the endless forests. It turns out all people along the rails think in Moscow time for train travel. One of our cabin mates says that even in the markets on the lake north of Irkutsk, just ask what time the train leaves for the next city and the answer will be in Moscow time, not local. The clocks on the trains are all set to Moscow time, and when the train pulls into the stations all across the many time zones this train crosses, the prompt on my cell phone asks if I want to switch to Moscow time, even when we are a third of the world away from Moscow.

I guess I should not find it strange that throughout the empire everyone is thinking about Moscow, knows what time it is in Moscow, has their attention for scheduling on Moscow time. Some say it makes it easier to travel since we are constantly going in and out of other time zones. No, it does not. But I haven't thought so much about Moscow as when I wonder what time it is, and I am not so sure that isn't the point.

Clearly, we are still adjusting, much like Chekhov when

he wrote home and said it would be a long journey. But by the time he reached Baikal, the deepest lake in the world, he wrote home again to his brother that he had little desire or need to return. And like Chekhov, we face the apparently familiar contrast of trying to hold on to familiar habits while being tugged toward this addicting landscape, away from our comfort zone, our homes, and our parents. I am not my father, nor are any of us. We spend our youth trying to break free from our parents' norms and expectations, and eventually we all manage it, one way or another; but sometimes even in my fifties I feel like I am *still* trying to break away. It is not hard to understand that we are always sons, even while raising our own children, until we lose our parents, and then our role on this journey becomes significantly more focused. I cannot tell if Michael has been trying to bust out on his own or not; we both took off for the far side of the world together—and I'm not sure that makes me a good father or not, but we find ourselves here, nonetheless. And so together we continue this adventure as we head toward Irkutsk and Lake Baikal on this self-imposed exile, this abandonment of reason.

Four

Persistence

This evening I write in the dining car, drink tea, and the only other passengers are an elderly man and his son, also drinking tea. They are quiet and both glance at me from time to time. Eventually, I gather the nerve to walk to their booth and ask if they speak English. The younger of the two—a well-dressed man about my age, speaks broken English and he waves to the empty spot next to his father, an elderly man older by perhaps thirty years, also well-dressed, with medals on his chest and a deep, long-healed scar on his forehead. I sit down. The younger man introduces himself as Dima; and the elderly man, Sergei, wears two or three medals on his green shirt, and I ask if one particular medal is the same as another I had seen in St. Petersburg, a medal received for bravery during the Siege of Leningrad. It is.

The dining car on the trans-Siberian railroad looks much like old Airstream-style diners in America, with booths along both sides, full size windows at each one with small curtains, and all are kept clean, with flowers, a napkin holder and place mats. At one end of the car is a bar with well drinks, a small variety of more expensive liquor on a higher shelf, and a generous selection of domestic and imported beers and soft drinks. The menu rivals the most common pub at home. Grilled chicken, hamburgers with French fries and other sides are available, as well as more complete dinners and some appetizers. Caviar, too, and salmon slices with toast, borscht, and traditional fare such as cabbage and sausages for tourists like us who wish to feel part of the landscape, and for locals whose daily diet includes such items anyway.

The prices are about the same as they would be at stateside diners but remain a bit pricey for Russians from the countryside, so they usually buy their food from the babushkas at the stops along the way. Seeing as how there are so few tourists, the booths are usually available, so Michael and I spend much of our time here, playing chess, eating, and working. Later in the evening that changes as the businessmen on board come here to drink and share stories, but for now, it is just the three of us.

Tonight the tender notices this sudden mixture of cultures and generations. This always smiling woman sits at her own booth near the bar with several pads spread about which apparently need her attention. From time to time she looks up, partly to see if we need anything and partly, it seems, to catch what she can of our conversation. She normally likes to play traditional music on the player whenever I sit down, but when she sees me join this veteran and his son, she puts on Shostakovich, and I note how excellent she is at her job. We all recognize it immediately and the old man smiles. Composer Dmitri Shostakovich wrote his Seventh Symphony, the Leningrad Symphony, in the forties and performed it for the first time to a packed theater in his besieged city of Leningrad, while Nazi bombs exploded in the background. Today in St. Petersburg's memorial Piskaryovskoye Cemetery, where nearly 700,000 people, mostly women and children who died during the siege, are buried, the composition is still played while thousands of people pay their respects. I have spent many Victory Days there, meeting veterans, offering them a carnation in thanks for their work back then, so it is an honor to share tea with this hero of the Great Patriotic War.

It would be negligent of any traveler, foreign or domestic, to make this journey without learning about and acknowledging the Blockade in Leningrad, the horrors of World War Two in that city, and the incomprehensible courage displayed by the citizens of what is now St. Petersburg, which the Germans bombarded for 900 days in an effort to complete Hitler's desire to "wipe Leningrad from the map." That history is this old man's youth; and the fact he survived and went on to raise a son is nothing short of miraculous.

And this is where the trans-Siberian railway and Russian history collide.

Some background:

The original name in Russia for the railway was the "Great Siberian Way," and it was only in the west we called it the trans-Siberian railway. At the World's Fair in Paris in 1900, the railway was an exhibit with the most extravagant interior cars on display and promoted as the "Ride of the Czars." While it was true the line from St. Petersburg to Yekaterinburg was indeed the rail for Czar Nicholas II and his family to seek refuge in their palace on the Iset River, the promotion at the Fair was misleading since from the start this railway mostly carried people to war. When Czar Alexander put his son Nicholas on the project, he did so with the assistance of Sergei Witte, a minister in the Russian government and confidant of the Czar. The heart of the empire was, indeed, in the western third of the country. St. Petersburg and Moscow were, and still are for that matter, the center of the Russian universe, and from the time of Peter the Great's ambition to create a "Window to the West," the powers-that-be focused their attentions there. But in the late 1800's, the government noted the potential resources available in the east, thinking Siberia might be an economic boon instead of simply a destiny for dissidents. At the same time, St. Petersburg had its eye on parts of Manchuria and moved forward with the rail to that destination under the pretense of trade; the truth is they eventually occupied the territory, a move which aggravated Japan who also wanted control of the area. Japan saw the TSRR as a tool of expansion and eventual invasion, which, of course, it was. Hence, the Russo-Japanese War in 1904. But the tracks were not finished yet, and troop movement in the area where roads even today are poor, meant ultimate defeat for Russia.

Still, they had their rail, which a few years later was completed to the Pacific port of Vladivostok. But Japan had its day, and instead of Russia using the railway to dominate the eastern Asian region, Japan did just that by defeating Russia's Pacific fleet and controlling territory they long wanted. Their rise to power anticipated the conflict in the Pacific which would be that part of the globe's World War Two.

During World War One, the United States had many economic interests in the region, not the least of which was a ton of weapons strewn north from Vladivostok along the rail. To protect those interests, President Wilson sent eight thousand US troops to the region—the only time US soldiers were stationed in Russia. The War in Europe would not be over for another three months, but in Russia, change was constant. The Mensheviks had ousted Czar Nicholas and replaced him with Kerensky, who the Bolsheviks quickly ousted, so the allies had no one with whom to work in eastern Asia. But it was during that short and welcome reign of Kerensky that the US took over the operation of the trans-Siberian railway, a move supported by the allies in Europe and seen as the spread of democracy the western world had hoped for. At the same time, however, the Bolshevik Revolution swept east literally following the tracks all the way to Vladivostok. The United States withdrew their interests and in a few short years the noble ambitions of the entire empire would quickly derail.

Josef Stalin took over the Soviet Union in 1922, a post he

would hold for thirty-one years. He longed for a railway across the polar region of Russia to expedite travel to the Far East. This "Dead Road" was built by "enemies of the people" of Russia. It is estimated that 300,000 prisoners worked on this project with a third of them dying in the brutal northern winters. The entire project proved short-lived, however, when the small part of the line which had been completed sank into the ice and snow. But Stalin understood the value of rail transport, and the pogroms started by the Czar to relocate Jews to eastern Russia were continued under his rule with the aid of the trans-Siberian railway further south. It was now possible to purge entire towns, exile anyone who so much as spoke about him without praise, as well as those who outwardly opposed the oppressive government. In fact, not many people during those years rode the railway by choice. It was a means for guards to get to work or to send prisoners east. The rail between St. Petersburg and Moscow remained a crucial route between what is considered the cultural capital in the north and the political capital an eight-hour ride south. And the cross-continental railway in 1990's post-coup Russia on became a means of transport for workers heading to and from a job, families going to a dacha, and the rare and idealistic tourist heading to Beijing or Vladivostok.

Aside from so much death associated with this transport, there is one glaring and essential exception when rail travel was, in fact, a lifeline in Russia: World War Two. A separate rail from the trans-Siberian route was built by hand every single winter during the war across the frozen Lake Ladoga just to the east of Leningrad to try and bring in supplies and bring out citizens of the city, which was besieged from September 8th, 1941, until January 27th, 1944. During that time nearly one and a half million people in the city—mostly women and children—died of starvation. And because of the invading Germans, factories were moved from the western part of the country to the most eastern reaches of European Russia, in the Ural Mountains, where more than three hundred plants were rebuilt close to the railway, mostly by the prisoner population.

Before me now, however, is a man who refused to leave Leningrad during the siege. I mention my understanding of his courage and struggle, and the old man smiles. He places his hand on my wrist and says, yes, he could have ridden the rail across the lake during that first winter—he was just a young teenager, and no one would have questioned it. But he chose to stay and help transport whatever food he could to the front line, which during the blockade was in every direction.

The tender brings a plate of salmon and bread which they share with me, and we drink more tea. Sergei dips some bread in his tea, and his son offers me salmon. We speak for quite some time about the rail, about Michael and I and our wild idea to see Siberia, and about their present journey to a Dacha to spend August. Eventually, I ask about his medal, about the war, and how much he remembers. Sergei takes a long bite of his bread and nods toward the plate of salmon. "Food was the most significant issue," says Sergei as Dima translates while he looks in despair at his father, clearly knowing what comes next. "Leningrad's population of dogs, cats, horses, rats, and crows disappeared as they became the main courses on many dinner tables. Nothing was off limits. People ate dirt, paper, and wood. The vast majority of casualties were not soldiers, but women and children."

This much I know already: The siege of Leningrad is political history as well as military history, yet it is also personal. It is the story of a child living on a few grams of bread, his mother making sure he only takes small bites throughout the day for fear if he eats it all at once he will surely starve to death. He will anyway, and the history of the siege of Leningrad must include the story of these women who survived, these sorrowful mothers, who had to grasp whatever sliver of hope they could that they would win in the end so to save their beloved Mother Russia.

The siege is one of the chapters in books about 20th-century atrocities; yet it is also the conversation over beers in a corner pub, where as late as the nineties when I first started coming here, most veterans still held back their emotions against the questions of the curious. Some allowed others to cross the line into their world, allowed them to suffer the starvation through stories and tears because they knew it might be the only way these great heroes, the defenders of Leningrad, will be remembered.

I recall a conversation I had once with a woman in St. Petersburg's Palace Square. She was fifteen during the siege when she had to pull a sleigh carrying the body of her sister, who had died of starvation. She made it to the graveyard and left her sister on the pile of bodies. Another there, Alexander, remembered how he would cut up a piece of bread once a day for his brothers. His parents had died of starvation some time earlier.

Nearly three million civilians, including nearly half a million children, refused to surrender despite having to deal with extreme hardships in the encircled city. Food and fuel would last only about two months after the siege began, and by winter there was no heat, no water, almost no electricity, and little sustenance. These citizens still had two more years of this to endure. Leningrad is at roughly the same latitude as Anchorage, Alaska. It gets cold.

During that first January and February, 200,000 people died of cold and starvation. Because disease was a problem, the bodies were carried to various locations in the city. Even so, people continued to work in the deplorable conditions to keep the war industries operating. When they were not working or looking for food and water, they were carrying the dead, dragging bodies on children's sleighs, or pulling them through the snow by their wrists to the cemetery.

One man said, "To take someone who has died to the cemetery is an affair of so much labor that it exhausts the last strength in the survivors. The living, having fulfilled their duty to the dead, are themselves brought to the brink of death."

But the people of Leningrad would not surrender. I met a woman named Sophia in a graveyard on the north side of the city. She had been an adolescent during the reign of Czar Nicholas II and thirty years later lost her husband and son during the siege. We sat on a bench, and she told me of her life, of her family, as if time had turned it into a hazy event she had heard someone talk about years earlier. Her hands were transparent, and she spoke of Leningrad as being a prisoner of war, with no rations and no electricity and little hope. The city became a concentration camp, its citizens condemned to death by Hitler.

But thousands of people were evacuated across Lake Ladoga via the famous frozen Doroga Zhinzni, the Road of Life. During warm weather, some were boated across, but in winter they were carried on trucks across the frozen lake under German fire and moved via the railway. Heading north was pointless; the Finnish Army, allied with the Germans since the bitter Winter War with the Soviets in 1939-1940, held the line there. But once across the lake, these very tracks took people further east until the rails simply could not run. When we stand between the cars and rumble along, listening to the clashing of metal beneath us, it is hard for me not to think of the thousands of starving citizens transported east, listening to the same sounds.

"We simply had nothing to eat." Starvation was the Nazi's objective. The blockade was a time during which one gauged success by being alive or not. Some survivors, however, tell of encounters with people who had such severe mental illness from disease and starvation that it had become unbearable. The accounts are sometimes spurious, but too many narratives contain too many parallel events to write them off as exaggerated. Several wrote of what became known as "blockade cannibalism," including the story of a boy who was enticed to enter someone's apartment to eat warm cereal.

One woman used one of her dead children to feed the others.

For nearly three years, Leningrad was under attack night and day, and almost half its population, including 700,000 women and children, perished. The Germans left the city of Peter the Great in ruins. Still, the Nazis could not defeat Leningrad. The people of the city to this day are most proud of that fact that.

The likes of that bravery and sacrifice will never be seen again.

During those years as well as a decade before and past Stalin's death in 1954, Soviet industrialization moved many citizens to the region stretching from Omsk to the Pacific, and the vast majority of these people worked in towns built for the sole purpose of some factory. But the most infamous use of the railroad during this dark period was to transport prisoners to the Gulag system. Prisoners in the penal system in Russia were tapped to exploit the natural resources in the mineral-rich east. It started officially in 1929, but just five years later, nearly half a million Soviet citizens with a prison term of three years or longer were loaded on these rail cars and transported to the Gulags. Five years after that, the camp population totaled more than two million. Some eighteen to twenty million inmates, while suffering the most inhumane conditions, facilitated the exploitation of timber and minerals in remote areas in slightly more than two decades. They also laid railroads which branched off of this one, constructed roads, secured dams, and worked in the factories and on the farms.

The veteran looks around and says more quietly as his son again translates, "Every single person on this train is connected to the war; either a grandparent or parent was killed, or less likely, survived. Everyone on this train is fortunate to be alive because of citizens of Leningrad under the most horrific conditions. I played a very small part, but I am glad I survived to be able to raise my own family." He smiles at his son, who places his own hand on his father's sleeve.

Today, war monuments dot the landscape. Most of them

honor veterans of the Great Patriotic War, but many as well for those who served in Afghanistan, the most notable being the Black Tulip memorial in Yekaterinburg, named for the ship which carried home the Soviet deceased. The monuments to the Siege of Leningrad, or the "Blockade" as Russians refer to those dark nine-hundred days, are numerous in St. Petersburg, of course, but they also spread surprising far to the east, following the tracks taken by those souls who managed to get out of the city under cover of a cold, dark winter. The same chance Sergei turned down, as his medal clearly shows.

I grew up during the age of the Evil Empire, the Red Menace. Siberia and Irkutsk might as well have been on the moon—I was never going. All I knew of this land when I was young was from playing RISK with my older brother. He usually won but I had fun moving my armies around the board, sometimes skipping from Alaska to Kamchatka, proving to me capture of the Russian coast was key in controlling the outcome. When Michael was growing up, we did the same thing. But it was not until I was much older that I learned something valuable: that miserable game screwed up my sense of geography. Siberia is not a country or a state, it is a region, like the American West or heading out to the Plains. Ian Frazier wrote Siberia is more of an idea than a place. Irkutsk is not a country but a city, and Yakutsk is not *east* of Siberia it is *in* Siberia. The Ukraine does not take up most of map, does not run from the Arctic to the Med, and does not replace Russia, which that Soviet era game completely left off the planet. Still, those faraway places in beautiful colors with brightly colored armies became mythical. In the end, I didn't have to move armies to travel to Siberia; no opponents waited across Parker Brother's boundaries. I didn't roll doubles. I didn't pick the wild cards. I just came here, and in doing so I wiped out decades of ignorance about these people over a cup of tea and some salmon slices.

The old man looks out the window into the dark evening,

and I can sense his mind has recessed into some sharp and tortured memories. His son leaves his hand on his father's and nods to me, indicating he sees I understand. We sit quietly like this for a long time, drinking tea, as the train rolls toward what's next.

Five

Comrades

Sometimes I wander through cars, pause in each one for a few minutes to gaze out the large windows and watch the wilderness slowly retreat. The often-dirty windows imply a cloudy day, but the small clerestory windows which usually remain open in the bathrooms help me to better see the blue sky, and after the occasional rain sweeps past, even the cabin windows or those running the length of the hallway get washed. My thoughts drift out into the landscape and it is not difficult to imagine myself out there, hiking the barren roads and meeting local people, sharing their soup, listening to what must be absolute quiet, save the train, of course. The fields and forests we pass have become companions; they are always right there, like our cabin mates, slightly beyond reach, a little past complete comprehension. When I am home and imagine this place, the wilderness, and the small villages, I am filled with apprehension and doubt about travel here. But standing here now looking out past dirt roads, small stores, and occasional groups of houses, it is all so unassuming and welcoming. Imagination both makes the trip possible and endangers it from the start.

Spending this time so close to people with such little ability to interact forces us to face our own judgments of others, our preconceived decisions as to their motives as well as their judgments of us. The unfortunate reality of Americans my age is the apprehension I carried here because of what I can only guess was a false narrative fed to us for decades, for generations, actually. From what I can tell, it was the same for our counterparts. Yet here we are, and I can only hope any questionable expectations they might have had of us are as shattered as mine are of them. In this great metaphor, all of us just want to get where we are going, enjoy the ride the best we can in the company of others, and in the end maybe have a good story to tell.

Like this one:

Alexander Ivanovich is our current cabin mate. He is the personification of Boris from the old *Rocky and Bullwinkle* cartoons, everything an American my age grew up believing a Russian man looked like, in his white tee-shirt over a healthy mid-section, bushy eyebrows, a strong, square chin, and the smell of alcohol. And while none of the Russians I have met in all these many years of traveling to St. Petersburg and Moscow resemble that stereotype, Alexander nails it.

When we first entered our cabin on what we now call the "Alex Leg" of the trip, he slept in his bed, a half-empty vodka bottle on the table and a crushed can of Baltika beer next to him. It was an intimidating sight. And when he awoke, the alcohol had clearly absorbed his inhibitions. Alexander speaks fast and strong, always smiling, pausing only to think of more to say, and this is continuous. Every so often he shoves a small glass at me and yells "Wodka Bob! Wodka!" and I laugh and the three of us manage to communicate in our native tongues, not understanding but talking anyway. Still, somehow through sign language, mixed diction, and a carload of guesswork, we have learned he drives a Kia, the jewelry he purchased on the platform at one of the stations is for his daughter who has two daughters herself for whom he bought some dolls, and his favorite train snacks include tea and dried fish which he gladly shares with us. We learn some Russian and he learns some English, and he is proud as hell when we all take pictures together. If our fourth cabin mate has anything to say, it does not appear he will have a chance so long as Alex is awake, which is ironic since the fourth man here is one of the rare Russians on board with some understanding of English.

In Russia, a person's name is a combination of his or her first name and a variation of the father's first name, used as the offspring's middle name. So I also know that Alexander's father's name was Ivan, hence Alexander Ivanovich. When he had first asked Michael his name, he repeated it to himself in Russian— Mikhail. Then he asked my name. He stared at me quite some time repeating, "Bob. Bob. Bob." Then he stared at Michael with a huge smile, pointed at him and said, "Ah! Mikhail Bobovich!" And so it is. He laughed and yelled, "Wodka, Bob! Wodka!"

Michael takes Alexander breaks by dodging into the dining car and playing chess with other, less intimidating drunk Russians. These businessmen love to challenge him in chess and nearly always lose. Part of it is the alcohol and part of it is Michael's ability to play, but I watched one day as they sat around my son, six of them, all laughing and drinking and telling stories and enjoying the passing of time, and I thought how here, in Siberia, a thousand miles from anywhere, we are all exiles together. Should we all suddenly end up living in a remote village on the edge of our disillusionment, I know we would become good friends, comrades, and I would at least know their names. Still, few of our traveling companions are on vacation and none of them is passing through. They come with a purpose and a destination, and nearly every one of them is from somewhere in Siberia. It is a fine reminder that Michael and I are outsiders here, immigrants from a foreign land. That fact merely encourages them to maintain a constant stream of attempts to talk to us, to help us understand and make themselves understood, and to assist us in any way they can. We truly felt welcome with these men, and finally a part of the community that can come from train travel. If one of us ever has a reason to need assistance, I am certain there will be no short supply.

Still, I cannot help but wonder what the hell anyone is doing out here.

Two and half centuries ago during the rule of Elizabeth, Peter the Great's daughter, Russia ended the death penalty and instead began the exile program where a free work force was created with prisoners of all sorts. At the start those sent were accused of mostly violent crimes or serious political dissent. But as the years went by smaller crimes made the cut, particularly in an attempt to populate Siberia to help protect the lands from the east. In the twentieth century simply being Jewish or writing one cryptic sentence in a letter about Stalin could have you exiled to some small Siberian village. Most of those men and women worked hard in mines, aiding the government in taking advantage of their natural resources, but many political prisoners were simply sent away to cut off their influence in the west where Czars and General Secretaries were weary of their words which could stir more than a few impressionable, dissatisfied minds. The Decembrists remain perhaps the most famous exiles, sent to Irkutsk where these former aristocrats set up shop and continued life without the luxuries of Opera, fine dining, and regal residences. They relied upon their own sense of humor to entertain friends, and they held nightly skits, played music, and told stories to get them through the long, dark winters. One exiled woman had been pardoned and returned to Moscow, where she wrote how she longed for her days in Irkutsk. She said she did not realize how much she possessed when she had nothing in Siberia. Sometimes we must let go to get a handle on things.

This has been true since the beginning of the march eastward. When Chekhov trekked to Vladivostok, he took note more than a few times of the people and places that made him feel more welcome than the finest characters in the most modern of houses. Michael and I share similar experiences. Most immediately, we have Alexander, whose breath can set fire. When he is sleeping, I return to the cabin and close my eyes to enjoy the quiet; I feel free and can abandon the turmoil and tethers of daily life. It is like a long sigh, like the whistle of a distant train, like the tide rolling gently away.

Then Alex wakes up.

Right away he wants his tea, and each time he wishes to share tea bags with us. Earlier when he discovered the samovar did not have hot water, with a laugh he exclaimed, in Russian, of course, "Fine! Since the tea is not forthcoming, let's have a philosophical conversation!" Our fourth friend, the mystery companion on the bunk above Alex, translated this and we laughed hard. Chekov! Our hungover Russian companion, half asleep with bloodshot eyes, was quoting Chekov. He brings such joy and rare friendship to our small room. We learn about each other through hand signs and weak language skills, and always we have each other laughing. Well, Chekov also wrote, "Even in Siberia there is happiness."

Alex's smile fades and he shakes the sleep from his head as he looks silently out at the rain hitting the window. His eyes seem filled with anxiety and doubt, and I can see he seems to have fallen deep into some place that scares him. His bare feet are calloused beyond care, and his skin burned dark, his arms and legs muscular despite the beer gut. Did he serve time in one of the gulags we passed? Is he a guard in one? A mechanic? A professor of Russian lit on summer break? He looks out and I wonder if he is nervous about seeing his daughter and granddaughters, the way he shows us their picture with such love wrapped in apparent apprehension; the way he stares at it a long time; the way he wants us to stare at it a long time. There is so much about him that reminds me of myself, so much about these people which reminds me of those I know and love at home. The common denominator is our raw emotions and our need to connect to others, whether it be in love, in friendship, or in his fleeting companionship on a some small part of a larger journey. We are the same.

It occurs to me that when he disembarks, I will never see this man again; that is the nature of travel, the essence of experience. I hope he remembers us. I know I can probably never remember most of these times, the names of places, which town had which pub. There is simply too much to absorb, we are saturated with experience. But there will always be space in my recollections for Alexander Ivanovich, the drunk Russian who made us feel more welcome and at home than anyone else along the route. Chekov is right; I could live here. I could spend long periods of time sitting around a table, telling stories, drinking, playing games and laughing long with Russian friends. We would toast life in an ancient corner of this vast and untamed wilderness.

In more than two dozen trips to Russia I had never asked anyone what he did for a living; and I do not recall anyone ever asking me, and certainly not out here on the railroad thousands of miles from anywhere. If people are inquisitive, they certainly have not revealed themselves. This was true as well when I was teaching in St. Petersburg. Certainly, at the college everyone knew, but at cafes or the market in brief conversations with people, who back in the nineties wanted so desperately to try their English, no one tried the standard language-tape question, "What is your occupation?"

Ironic really, since it is one of the first questions we ask strangers in America. At home we are almost defined by our occupation; I am the "writer" or the "professor," and all other inquiries such as family ties or which house is mine are secondary at best. But here, my profession does not seem relevant to casual conversation. Here, I am "the dad traveling with his son" and we are, of course, "the ones from Spain." Well, that is fine. I would rather be defined as Michael's dad than anyone else's teacher anyway. At the very least, our friends on board seem to understand priorities. I can never be quite sure any lessons Michael might have picked up from me or possibility still latches on to are good examples or not, but I am certain that in our travels he has been witness to and a participant in a montage of customs and enough cultural variety to understand the value of inclusion, the benefit of withholding judgment, and how much we all need each other.

But I still want to know what people along this rail do for a living, so I look it up. About ten percent of Russians work in agriculture and another twenty-seven percent in industry, and since there aren't a lot of white-collar companions either on the railway or in Siberia, I am guessing we're surrounded by mostly working-class people, even here in second class. Siberia is very much a binary society. It is either city, like in Irkutsk or Vladivostok, with cafes and theaters and banks and festivals, or it is desolate, random farmers' shacks or gutted gulags scattered through the wild landscape.

I talked to one man who has decent English when he is not drinking and playing chess, and he strikes me as a businessman, which would explain his command of the language. He is the first, in fact, to tag us as Americans. Yet, he left at one of the more remote stations. It almost seemed cruel to leave him alone since the station is a small, royal blue shack with seemingly no roads or paths. How does one breach that topic? "Is that his office?" "His home?" "His punishment?" Maybe it is my cold-war mentality hemorrhaging on occasion, but clearly not asking is expected. The older travelers probably assume from *their* cold-war youths that I am some left-wing leftover looking for remnants of Emma Goldman or Jack Reed. American tourists simply cannot be found in the remote regions of Siberia. In fact, for tourists on board on this leg, it is only the two of us, a French family and a woman from the Netherlands traveling alone to who knows where for who knows why. She's the only other traveler with a solid command of English and I would talk to her, but she sleeps all the time.

We had one cabin mate for a short bit earlier in this leg of the trip who looked precisely like actor Liam Neeson. Same height, same face, and to add to the mystery, he wore a Nike warm-up suit and running shoes and had a Russian military tattoo on his wrist. He was pleasant and quiet with a small constant sardonic smile which made me all at once feel safe from outsiders and foolish to be in the same cabin; his kind of quiet felt somewhat disconcerting, and I started to imagine he was "assigned" to our cabin to keep an eye on the two Americans, one of whom had already made twenty something trips to Russia and "says" he is a professor, the other constantly taking pictures. To each other we called him Liam, and while he never spoke more than the cordial good morning and how are you in Russian, his small smile when Michael and I talked to each other indicated to me he was probably quite fluent in English. I wish I had spoken more to him, had managed to work out communication between us the way we have with Alex, using the rudiments of language, but like everywhere else in the world, some people's walls seem stronger than others, and his body language indicated his walls were not coming down. I certainly have learned to pick and choose with whom I am willing to risk what has more than a few times become a linguistic bloodbath.

Perhaps they ask each other what they do for a living but find it too personal for foreigners. To be fair, growing up I didn't even ask my own father what he did for a living. I mean I knew his occupation, but I never inquired about his day, about what took place. Part of me was too busy growing up or playing with friends, and part of me did not want to bother him after he had been doing it all day. But those are adult responses when I wonder why I did not ask, and the truth is at ten years old I probably simply didn't care. He did his thing, and I did mine. His thing made my thing possible but even that was too complicated to contemplate when I was ten, so we talked about baseball.

In the States I hear so many recall their youth without a dad present, as if the man was never there or emotionally estranged, or the younger one was just too rebellious to be around all that much. But that was not the case with my father and me. We got along fine; we just did not talk a lot because of our circles. My circles crossed paths with friends, sometimes with siblings, obviously my mother. His circles crossed paths with colleagues or neighbors, or us when on the golf course or watching baseball, but even then, the conversation was about playing golf or ball. This was also a generational thing; particularly the gap between the "greatest" generation and the "baby boomers." This was old school; this was adults and kids being themselves separately, and between those two generations lay one of the widest gaps in American social history. That was not necessarily true in our home, but I never asked about his day, and now I'm sorry for that. I wish I had. As adults we remained close, and it seems Sergei and Dima have as well, but I cannot help but wonder if they, too, stayed in separate circles roughly the same time period as my father and I on the other side of the world.

I guess you have to be a parent to understand what kind of child you were. You need a basis of comparison that goes beyond the parent-child relationships of cousins or friends. It must be later, years later, when you understand what he would have wanted you to ask, what he wished you had shown interest in, how close—or not close—you were. Turns out we were so much closer than I knew, and I could have asked anything, but I never did.

And now as we roll along, I wish I had asked all the people I have met so far what they do for a living, but they've all disembarked, and I have learned to carry a slight resignation on this trip that anywhere we go and anyone we meet will be fleeting, and we will not—will absolutely not—return. And there's the metaphor. That is even more reason to risk a little invasion of my own, pull the journalist out of my tool bag and see what stories I might expose.

Yes, of course. These are one-way tickets; and we are all merely temporary companions. And we know, I mean we have an absolute conviction, that we always inquire too late, walk away wishing we had put ourselves out there and asked the tough questions, showed more love, risked being ourselves. Instead, our literal and proverbial train rolls along and we stare out the window at an endless forest of birch trees.

Well, anyway, speaking Russian gives me a headache and no one from St. Petersburg to Vladivostok on this railroad save the French family and the sleeping Dutchwoman speaks anything but Russian, and some of them nearly unintelligibly. Every word must be unlocked before moving on. Add to that the multiplicity of each English word and clearly a simple conversation is akin to a non-English speaker trying to decipher a Shakespearean monologue.

It is why I take breaks and walk through the cars to gaze at the landscape, this treacherously beautiful landscape. These fields of Siberia are saturated with wildflowers, green and yellow and red, and the smallest of royal blue or stark yellow buildings is beautiful against what can only be a bleak winter landscape. Today, however, it is nearly eighty degrees outside, and close to that inside when they choose to not turn on the air conditioning.

Outside in one shack surrounded by birch trees, a guard with a gun stands alone, hundreds of miles of nothing both going and coming back; I can only suppose for some local military installation. Further east, gulags or factories or other such buildings stand taken over by wilderness and wear. The barbed wire is broken and the walls long ago crumbled. The vast majority of Russia is wide-open wilderness of forests and plains, agricultural lands and lakes. It is too warm in the summer to maintain the familiar title of "Frozen Wasteland," but it is not difficult to see that once the first frost arrives, moving around is nearly impossible. The only road across Siberia freezes during the winter, and people for the most part will stay where they are.

Rarely in life do we wake, spend the day in conversation and observation and contemplation, and then return to sleep without any need to check social media, voice mail, and even less need to know where we are. It gives me a lot of time to think. We are in a culture so distinctly different than our own. Out here beneath the eastern stars, I am trying my best to be a father, farther away from the shadow of my own father, but in doing so I am seeking him out in the corners of the car, hoping to catch a wisp of his breath on the back of my neck reminding me what to do, even when I am doing okay. I thought I saw a piece of him in the old man in the dining car, then again at one of the stops in the eyes of a man checking under the carriages, banging a metal rod against the tracks. When we start looking for familiar faces this far from home, I figure there must still be something back there we need, perhaps some semblance of security. But I imagine we cannot have that kind of peace of mind until we first let go and allow ourselves to trust strangers, and even to trust each other a little bit more. I cannot tell if being a father has made me a better son or being my father's son has made me a better father. But here we are on the edge of something new, both of us learning how to let go, in Siberia of all places.

According to the movies we should be murdered or kidnapped or lost. We love to create terror when we do not know or understand a place except through old falsehoods. And I suppose the people who come to our country for the first time, who have trouble with the language, who want to experience and know and see, are terrified, drowned in the horror stories and mysteries created by some need to fill in the white space of not-knowing. It is then we hope someone, some stranger who has faith in us, helps us carry that cross until we are on our feet.

We haven't been out here long, but we have been out here long enough to know we can rely upon any single one of these men to lend us a hand should we need it, and I wonder now if my frustration is borne out of my desire for them to know that they can trust us as well, that if they need us for anything, they need only ask, and I'm not just slightly irritated that I don't think they know that. I want them to understand that except for the language we are the same, very much the same.

Six

Dialogue

One afternoon I sit in the café waiting for Michael who runs back to our hotel to get his camera. I order tea and watch the people about stir and settle back down, talk and then sit quietly, except for one man with a beard trying hard to look like Dostoevsky. He even has a few books in his open case and a few pens in the pocket of his shirt. I sit at the next table.

"I heard you talking to the other one. Is he your son?"

"He is. He's upstairs getting his camera."

"Yes, he looks like you. I heard you talk about the train. You are going how far?"

"Vladivostok."

"Oh, so far! You are not going to Beijing? Most tourists go to Beijing."

"No, we want to stay in Russia the whole way."

"Why?"

"I am writing about the trip. And my son is taking pictures."

"You are a writer? Then you must be a professor, a teacher of children maybe?"

"Ha, yes a professor."

"Yes, Good. All writers are professors, especially if you can take the time to travel across Russia, no?"

"I suppose that is true. Your English is good."

"Thank you. I am from Moscow, but I taught at St.

Petersburg University. Right now I am traveling a bit. You are from the United States?"

"Yes. I've taught at Baltic State though."

"Ah, yes, the Technical University. Very good. Would you like a shot of cognac in your tea?" He pulls out a small flask and adds some to his own and invites me to his table, and then he pours some cognac into my tea and we toast with the tea and sip. The cognac cools off the tea and it is easier to drink and now has some kick. "In Russia either you drink because you have no money or you drink because you're the only one who does. Which one are you?"

"Both, I suppose. Taught? You are retired then?"

"Retired! Ha, yes, well, I suppose so. They retired *me*, I suppose."

"What did you teach?"

"Ah, another good question! If you ask me, I will say Math. But if you ask my administrator, he will tell you I taught Philosophy." He looked around at the people and then up at the sky, then down as his cup. "I suppose I, how do you say it? stumbled. I take it one moment each now. Our Chekhov did say, after all, 'The university brings out all of our abilities, including our incapability.'" He took a sip and sighed. "And you? What is it you teach? Math maybe?"

"English, art, literature. Humanities."

"Ah, yes, a renaissance professor, yes? I thought maybe math because of Baltic State."

"I taught as a guest in the Languages department there."

"Let me guess. Pushkin."

"Ha, yes."

"And Dostoevsky."

"Correct."

"And what about Gogol? You must teach Gogol! And Akhmatova."

"Anna, yes, but not Gogol."

"Ah, well, that is a shame. Gogol is my favorite. Do not tell me you teach Chekhov. No one understands Chekhov!" he says with some anger, like a writer upset that critics misinterpreted his work.

"No Chekhov but I *am* reading him. *Journey to the End of the Empire.*"

"Yes! Such a perfect choice. Yes."

"How do you like Turgenev?"

"Yes! *Fathers and Sons*! My own father gave me a copy once many years ago! A wonderful memory! Thank you!"

"A good work."

"Yes, good!"

"And Pasternak?"

"Oh, first rate! In Moscow schools I had to memorize some of his poems, and am glad for having had to do so. Have you read him in Russia? I hope you read his poems in Russian someday! He is as good as Pushkin, I think. They are different than the translations. Did you know his translations of Shakespeare are still the ones we use in Russia today?"

"That's incredible. I hope to read his poetry in Russian someday," I say, and add, "How about *Doctor Zhivago*?"

He drinks the rest of his laced tea and looks around, sighs. A small smile behind his grey beard tells me he his frustrated but holding his tongue. I do not understand, exactly. "It is a beautiful day out. I hope you and your son, who I imagine is the young man approaching now, have a safe and fine journey." He stands up and so do I. He turns to me, takes a deep sigh, and nods. "I read it once, when it first came out here in Russia in the late 1980s. In St. Petersburg you met Lara, no? As you head east you will meet Tonya. Then, professor, reread Mr. Pasternak's *Doctor Zhivago*." He adds, "Dasveedanya," nods to Michael, and walks away, turning once as if he wishes to add something, but then he is gone.

I watch him walk away looking every bit a man older than

his years as my youthful son stands next to me ready to continue this journey. I think of Pasternak: "I don't like people who have never fallen or stumbled. Their virtue is lifeless and of little value. Life hasn't revealed its beauty to them."

I make a note to read *Doctor Zhivago* again when we return home.

Seven

The Metaphor

For quite some time now, my rarely-tapped-into conservative side has suggested it is time to talk to my son about what is next in his life, career-wise I mean, time-to-think-of-the-future wise. All parents go through this with their children, I suppose. It is not so necessary to discuss their plans if something about their lives indicates forward motion. "I'm going to college" works well, even if one lacks a certain effort. "I've started my own computer business and am working on selling it to Google," is another preferred response. And because we are spending the summer riding a metaphor—truly, nothing symbolizes forward motion more than a train barreling across two continents—I have decided to interrupt our focus on the present to discuss the future. Somewhere along the line it should not be difficult to digress into something like, "Hey, what are your plans?" I knew before we left that this would happen, that horrific but predictable conversation all fathers have with their sons about security and ambition.

My own father asked me once over brunch during my senior year of high school. I told him I wanted to take a year off and then go to college. I timed my response so his mouth was full and he could not answer right away to give me a chance to make my case. I suppose he already knew what I really wanted to do was travel, figure out how to pay for that instead of following some forgettable path. But his generation had a completely different set of parameters than mine. His was World War Two; his was college for the privileged only; his was the Andrew Sisters and Boys Town; it was a time when dressing down meant loosening the tie.

My generation is the Beatles, the Stones, Run DMC; my generation is Vietnam and Masters' degrees; flip flops and adventure travel. And ironically enough, my generation has somehow culturally bled into my son's generation—the same adventurous ambitions, the same music and foods, the same clothes even. Maybe that is why both of us adjusted to the railway quickly, feeling comfortable far from home, ordering drinks and shelving responsibility. He quickly took to this lifestyle; I cannot imagine why.

Michael spends much of this time with his camera, shooting photographs of the trees in a wilderness so vast that even crossing it by train seems an impossibility. I watch him at the windows watching nature—both untamed. We sit in the dining car and I write in my journals, but my mind is elsewhere. At one point he turns to me and says, "Throw Mama from the Train." Just like our attempts to trump each other by naming train-songs, we have been trying to name all the movies we can which include great train rides. We came up with some good ones too: *Doctor Zhivago, Murder on the Orient Express, The General, The Ghost Train, North by Northwest, the Polar Express, The Taking of Pelham 123,* and a few scary flicks, including *Trans Siberian.* We have long talked about the artistry involved in film making—the need for narrative, the entirely separate art form of a cinematographer's eye, and the music so essential for tone. I make a note in my journal that it was probably while first watching *Murder on the Orient Express* that I believed I would take a long train ride someday. My father's daily treks by train to and from Wall Street did nothing to inspire me to follow him into a broker's career in the city, but the sound of the train leaving so early instilled in me some sense of adventure.

My own father never dreamed of Russia—the Soviet Union. His generation defended liberty against the Nazis and the Japanese, returned from World War Two to settle down and make sure their children did better than they did. He set us an example of the American work ethic, built us a house in the suburbs, insured us a college education, and watched us build lives and families of our own in the tradition of the Great American Dream. But when I was young, for Christmas every year he bought me those books I read again and again and then passed them on to Michael: *Bound for Glory, The Boy Who Sailed around the World Alone*, and *A Walk across America*. So at brunch that morning in high school when he swallowed his food and had a chance to answer, I could tell he already knew what I was going to say. As a father, he out-dad's me ten to one.

I watch Michael at the window take pictures of small graveyards in the forest, practicing his art in a land whose history has most often been underscored by artists like Tolstoy, Eisenstein, and Pushkin. My son is an artist as well; I can tell by the way he does not point and shoot but rather frames what he sees, waits for the sun, or waits for the clouds depending upon the mood, the character, the narrative. His predecessors include Alexey Trofimov, whose current collection includes award-winning, minimalist work to make the most citified folks find reason to ride to Siberia. Most famously, though, is the work of V.L. Metenkov, whose house is now a museum celebrated by National Geographic. As for the Russian landscape painters, Alexei Savrasov might be the most celebrated, even if the volume of his work was criticized by his colleagues for not having enough social commentary. Russia is most certainly a land of artists, and social realism was so alive during the Stalin era, it is not surprising such sentiment leaked through. The people I have met in this country are so much more intensely aware of what is going on around them than in the States, that social commentary is always just around the next conversation.

Throw some artists into the mix, a group which already dips its brush in commentary, and you have unearthed the Russian art community.

If Michael's work has any commentary at all, it is to speak of the world as virgin despite its history, tranquil despite its wars, accessible despite its isolation. Some planning was involved to come to a place where I find myself having a drink in a rolling pub while my son stares at the green hills and white trees, interrupted by the occasional graveyard or dilapidated shack, but in the end, it was as simple as pointing ourselves in the right direction.

I want to tell him to defy his desire to wander and instead figure it out on the way to a degree. I need to insist he go to college, secure a job. And I am painfully aware there is no way for me to breach this subject without sounding hypocritical. I certainly do not want to tell him the truth: that if I were his age again and had it to do over, I would wander longer, avoid the main current my friends followed and cut my own course. I would not be in a hurry; but I would not sit around. Still, as a father I want my son to be secure, to be stable in an unstable world. So I know the only way to have this conversation, the only way for it to be truly honest and open, is to talk in the dining car over vodka. If we are going to talk about his future, one of us has to be drinking.

So after a while we settle down together in a booth and listen to balalaika music the tender puts on and I decide it is time to talk. It also occurs to me that this conversation should be a celebration, not a lecture. I order a beer and a shot of vodka and at my suggestion Michael does the same. I tell him we never had a proper "kicking off" celebration since boarding the train in St. Petersburg. We are on a roll east toward an eventual six thousand miles. Whenever someone asks where we are going, and we say Vladivostok, they react with surprise and admiration, as if it is a city only heard about in mariner's tales or old, Russian folk tunes, and I suppose to most of them it must be. There is something enticing about traveling farther across their homeland than most of these men probably ever will. But here we are, and it seems as good a time as any to both celebrate and talk. The only other passengers are four men eating dinner. The dining car attendant is a robust woman with traditional clothes and apron who sits at her own booth going over paperwork and drinking coffee.

She brings us our drinks and asks if we want anything else, so I open the menu and I ask for a tray of cucumbers and tomato slices and then some caviar with bread. She smiles wide, nods at our shots and beers, and puts her hand up to stop me from ordering more; apparently, she catches on and makes her own suggestions. She points to the borscht and I nod and put up two fingers, and then she suggests the smoked salmon strips. Michael and I relax and listen to music and toast our good fortune to be in Siberia, and we toast the unknown which brought us here to begin with, that finds us—father and son—barreling along the tracks into wherever is next.

The food comes out and we drop a dollop of sour cream in the soup and toast again with another vodka, compliments of Irina the attendant, and she smiles and laughs and says, "Na Zdorovie!" She puts on different Russian folk music with accordions and a chorus, and the four men toast our celebration, and the entire car becomes ours, and we make that essential step from observers to participants in this foreign and all-absorbing culture, so that it seems somewhere east of Yekaterinburg already nearly seven thousand miles from home, we begin our journey.

Michael is quiet for some time, and when the food is gone, we order tea and he looks out the window at the darkness save some random houses and non-stop stations, all illuminated by the light pouring out of the train cars. This is the time to talk, I decide. We are here now.

I am thinking of the right words. It is not that I have trouble talking to him about anything; I don't. It is just that I want to balance the need to ask his thoughts about his plans to move forward in life—his philosophy of sorts, his game plan—but I don't want to break this spell we are under as travelers, companions. We are both artists, attempting to express ourselves through our own mediums, and here I sit speechless trying to say something fatherly.

He looks out the window and says this reminds him of the train scene in the movie *Out of Africa*, where Meryl Streep is crossing the vast wilderness toward a new life. I look at my son, and while I do not doubt my father's pride for me, it couldn't possibly match mine for Michael at this moment. I have never seen a person so aware, so completely in the moment, as Michael looking out the window. What's next? I think. Isn't that what we are going to talk about? He leans forward so I can hear him over the music and says, "That movie has my favorite line in it. Near the end just before he leaves for that last flight, Redford says to Streep, "I don't want to wake up one day at the end of someone else's life." He glances back outside, nodding to himself and I remain quiet a moment.

Talk over.

I never said a word, just like my Dad. We invite the others in the dining car to join us and the attendant brings six bottles of Baltika and we play chess and laugh and come to life in the dead of night a thousand miles from nowhere crossing one of the planet's most barren and wild lands.

While Michael plays against the businessman, I realize I cannot look at this land without my mind spiraling into the world of art and artists—writers, painters, musicians, photographers, dancers. Artists all. I have traveled with many people to Russia, but always to St. Petersburg and Moscow and always as a professor, never like this, as a father and a writer without the comfort of the flood of western influence in those cities, and I never before ventured this far east. But some years ago, an artist friend of mine, James Cole Young, insisted I bring him to Russia. He was a landscape artist heavily influenced by Casper Friedrich and Isaak Levitan, whose sweeping style in his pastoral paintings inform Cole's paintings of clouds.

"Kunzinger! Bring me to Russia!" he said in his signature I-already-have-my-passport style of planning.

"Okay. Where?"

"All of it, St. Petersburg, Moscow, Siberia, anywhere I can paint without being bothered!"

We talked it out for a while, but he was not feeling especially well, and his health deteriorated until eventually he died of lung cancer before we had a chance to fulfill that dream of his. That would have been the end of it, but like many artists, often their strongest influence comes after death. A few years later, Cole's widow, Sharon, called and said she wanted to bring Cole to Russia and that I had to be the one to bring her there.

So we went. It turns out carrying human remains on an airplane doesn't violate any TSA regulations, so Sharon poured some of Cole into a sandwich baggie and put him in her purse behind her sunglasses. A few days later, we stood near the gift shop in the Hermitage Museum in St Petersburg, Russia, ready to place part of the late artist among some of his legendary influences. "Well, we made it," Sharon said, as I studied a map of the galleries looking for German artists.

"Not yet," I said. "Security at the airport has nothing on these hounds watching the paintings." I looked closer at the map. "Ah, found him. Let's go."

Cole Young's paintings of the sky, of landscapes, blur the line between reality and representation. Stare long enough and you become part of the cloud, part of nature. One autumn day on his western New York farm, we had been talking about traveling to Russia when he said, "They have a painting there I must see which is one of the works which inspired me to paint—Casper Friedrich's 'Memories of the Riesengebirge.'" I know the work. This landscape he loved has details and depth like many of Cole's own early landscapes, and in several reviews my friend was compared to the German artist.

"We'll do the whole art thing, Kunzinger! You write and I'll paint! All artists should go to Russia at some point! I don't think people paint the Russian landscape anymore." We talked about it most of that night and for weeks after, but he fell ill. Sharon knew what she wanted to do, and we stood outside the gift shop, me with the map, Sharon with the baggie of Cole.

We wound our way through the maze of rooms to the hall of German artists. A few friends joined us to distract the guard in her chair at the entrance to the otherwise completely empty gallery.

"Here it is," I said, and we stood before Friedrich's work. One of our friends conveniently asked the guard directions to some difficult to find gallery while another friend and I stood between Sharon and the guard, blocking the view. Sharon carefully poured some of Cole in her hand and dusted the inner frame and canvas with ashes. It was part timeless and part creepy.

Then she took my palm and poured Cole into my hand. I laughed. "He hated when people touched him," I said, and Sharon laughed hard. "Oh my God, that's right!"

But I stood gripping Cole, looking at the landscape, loosing myself for a moment in the depth of the countryside. I thought of my college days, sitting in the studio until four am listening to John Lennon and talking to Cole about life and death and watching him scrape off some tree in his painting which had to move for better depth. We were so young, but we talked endlessly about art and about nature, and how a canvas can capture the beauty of time and keep it there, permanent, untouched by age or fading memories, and how photographs and good writing can do the same.

Our lives were saturated by innocence. The pastoral land-scape of southwestern New York made artists of us all. Cole painted, and we played guitars or sat on his porch where he would often hold court to complain about useless, wasted time or people's poor taste in art. Years later he said to me, "Those were great days back then, weren't they?" They were.

I stared at my palm. My friends urged me to hurry as the guard was growing suspicious, but I stood wondering which part of Cole I held. I imagined I held his hand, so long and tender, yet strong. His taught muscles held tight to brushes his entire life, painted masterpieces which hang all over the world. I decided I held that hand in mine, and I moved it slowly toward "Memories," and blew gently enough to watch the ashes land in the crevices of the canvas, dusting the mountains, easing some onto the frame.

"They'll clean this up," I said, "but some will remain."

Sharon smiled. "I suppose. But for now he is here among artists," she said. I watched some ash settle to the floor and thought how a part of anyone who travels to Russia is always left behind. On the way out, I stopped in a restroom to wash my hands and thought how Cole will forever be part of the landscape. *How long*, I wondered, *before this water washes into the river, moving further into nature.*

Now, I look at Michael who sits and smiles, trying his best to talk to our friends sitting around trying their best to talk to us, passing the time as we pass small royal-blue shacks and yellow stations through the night. Others enter the car, and a small boy about eight is at the next booth sitting next to his father who is reading a book. The boy is toying with his fries and staring at his dad. Every once in a while, he reaches up with a fry and without looking his father bites it, smiles down at him, and continues reading. They seem content in this apparently familiar routine. I do not think the father is hungry as his plate still has food, but his son seems satisfied every time the man bites a bit of a fry.

Most of these passengers are engaged in their ongoing lives, as this seems routine to them. But for newbies like Michael and me, and perhaps this young boy, we absorb the landscape both inside and out with every sense we have. I realize that in our daily lives we often stare down at the ground. We look at our shoes, or at the sidewalk cracks or the leaves near the curb, or at the wrappers and trash left on the lawn. Maybe we do not look up and around too much because it is too much to take in. We are too focused on the trivial, which alone can be overwhelming. Apparently, it is the same in Russia. The young boy, like us, is engaged in life around him, while the regulars read a book. I wonder how much of this trip he will remember, which makes me curious about how much my own son will recall as he ages. And me? What will I look back at and conjure up with perfect clarity, and which moments have already escaped between cars, left behind as we move forward? Will Alexander Ivanovich hear some English spoken and think of us, of those days in the compartment drinking tea and laughing? I wonder again how much of me will stay in Russia. There will be moments, however, for which I will require a photograph or a painting to recall the details; perhaps some descriptive paragraph to again appreciate the Siberian soul.

Sometimes when we are traveling in a strange land, after the initial wonder wears away, our minds return to their natural state and we find comfort in some routine from home, like reading, or perhaps simply looking around but not noticing so much as our thoughts are seven-thousand miles away. It can be exhausting to maintain the enthusiasm and staggering newness of some foreign soil, but I am determined to take it all in, so I sit here in the dining car and realize that Cole was right, as was Bob Shacochis: all artists should go to Siberia at some point in their lives.

Eventually, I thank the woman who works at the bar for

all of her help. She wipes the counter and smiles, and when I offer her a tip for all she did, she refuses a few times before accepting. We return to the cabin and write in our journals and talk quietly about what a great day it has been: we made good friends and celebrated with them and we hardly had to speak a word the entire time. We laughed a lot, we used hand signals, and when we could we spoke in bad Russian. Little was lost in translation. It was a string of pure moments, of white birches against a dark-green forest, of the soft rumbling of the train, of the slightly anxious apprehension we both felt when a drunk man first approached about playing chess, and the gathering of men and the fields of Siberia saturated with wildflowers, green and yellow and red, and the buildings painted royal blue. We were far from home. We were as far from home, in fact, one can get before heading back. GPS is worthless here. Maps are of little value.

This is why we came. This is why we are here. To end up in Vladivostok, yes, but also to end up at each station along the way, to find perspective and discover the symmetry in our own world, and, along the way, not find ourselves on anyone else's journey but our own.

Eight

Check Mate

In the early 1990s, the International Herald Tribune reported about gangs on the trans-Siberian Railroad. They formed mostly in the east, on the Chinese/Mongolian border, and from time to time they terrorized passengers on the route running through Mongolia to Beijing. One story circulated of gang rapes, mass abuse, and outright stealing everything on board from everyone's cabin. The women who worked the cabins at the time were reported to be either too scared to do anything or paid to look the other way. In either case, the famous ride celebrated by travel writers and Russophiles the world over started to acquire a questionable reputation. Tourists fled to other places just when communism had ended, which only increased the crime since there were fewer witnesses and virtually no government prosecution on either side of the border.

By the time we boarded this train, most of the crime has become petty; people pillaging through suitcases, picking up passports and rubles while passengers are in the dining car or the bathroom. Normal, predictable theft which mostly affects the inexperienced travelers who do not know to keep the important papers and money with them or secure their baggage in the compartments under the beds, which while they can be accessed by anyone, are very difficult to do quickly, so most thieves look elsewhere. But every once in a while, travelers can get lazy or tired or overconfident in the trust we place in newfound friends when riding together in a small cabin for days at a time. Then there is a cultural aspect: We are used to infinitely more personal space in the United States, but in Russia, particularly for those without as many resources, being together with all your stuff in close quarters is not unusual. Sometimes it can be difficult to decipher when someone is simply being themselves, used to such cramped quarters, and when someone is bleeding just a little too far into your personal space. In addition, when you live together like this for a few days, particularly since few travelers remain on board for any longer than that and don't get to know you at all, it is necessary to understand that these strangers can watch your every move, take note of what's in your bags, where you keep your funds, how long it takes to eat, go to the bathroom, how long you spend between cars playing music and getting lost in the landscape, how long you spend writing in the dining car two carriages away.

Add to this the cultural reality that being overly cautious around people apparently contradicts how to act in rural Siberia. So we make an extra effort to be part of our surroundings, talk to others and share whatever stories we can piece together.

I read a story just before we boarded about two men who walked through one of the trains going car to car stealing people's money. They started an hour before one of the arrivals at a busy stop and worked their way through, finishing just as the train pulled in. They were gone. No one dare chase them for fear of missing the train's departure time, forcing them to purchase a new ticket which surely would amount to more than the rubles stolen. Needless to say I was careful of where we kept out valuables. I just assumed someone else might be waiting for me to let my guard down, perhaps while having drinks in the dining car, late at night. Or while I am writing.

Or playing chess.

Michael retrieves his chess set from the cabin and we play a few games when a man in the foursome at the next booth asks Michael if he can play along. The man sits in our booth next to me and politely puts two pieces in his hands offering them to Michael to choose. It takes seven moves for Michael to checkmate the man with his queen, protected by his bishop, though in the Soviet days the bishop was called the "officer," as this man calls him.

Michael is pretty good, and this dude is pretty drunk, so the next few games go the same way, just not as fast since the man's friends join him, lean over him, and give advice. Sometimes he listens and other times he brushes them off with a smile. He looks like a Russian version of actor Bruno Kirby, and he laughs easily which keeps the mood light. Eventually, four loses later, he bows out and one of his friends, the one with the best advice though it usually went unheeded, takes over, and while the game lasts quite a long time—longer than the previous games combined—the Russian eventually wins.

By the time the second or third chess game with this man is underway, other travelers gather in other booths talking to each other, laughing, watching, so the different conversations surround us with a festive atmosphere in the Russian night as we roll into the dark and they order another round. Then another.

Michael plays a few other people, and friends of theirs gather and laugh and poke fun at their companions for losing so easily. When Michael said, "check" to one opponent, the man got up and ran out of the car. We all laugh, and we all have a great time as others come and go, sometimes to watch, sometimes to offer advice, and always to drink. But also always someone is missing. At first, I do not think about it, and when I do notice I simply figure it because of the crowds already in the dining car. But at some point, my guard goes up. I lose track of those traveling together and realize I have been so engaged with the game, I am not paying attention to life around me. It is easy to become absorbed in this culture.

I wonder if our cabin is okay, and our tickets, our money, and other materials. I tell Michael I will be right back when an uproar rises from the table as Michael takes down his opponent's queen. My panic increases when I realize, despite Michael's fine ability to play, he wins against these men far too easily, and the Russians encourage him to continue with just too much enthusiasm. I excuse myself and head through the cars toward our cabin.

When I arrive, our two cabin mates are on their beds watching a movie on a laptop, so I say hello and poke around like I am looking for something, trying not to seem suspicious and at the same time trying not to give these guys a tour of our valuables. Eventually, I am satisfied everything is fine and feel stupid for my suspicions, so I close and secure our belongings and return to the table where Michael remains completely engrossed in a game with the last player, laughing and communicating in the universal language of Chess.

The first player walks back to the booth from the bar with three shots of vodka, hands two to Michael and me, and he toasts his "New American friends." He tells us it is refreshing to meet Americans. He tells us he was raised to be suspicious of Americans and he always thought that to be wrong, and he is happy to be able to tell his father in Irkutsk everything he had learned about us was false. "My new American Mates!" he exclaims, raising his shot. And he leaves. When I walk to the bar to pay the bill, the woman says the man already took care of the tab for the evening.

Nine

Poorer People

On a station platform one evening in the cool, night air, I walk up and down the length of the cars until I come to the third-class carriages. This section of the train seems more akin to a bus on wheels which carries people either on a strict budget or those who have such a short ride, paying more for unnecessary comfort is a waste of difficult to come by cash. The romantic in me wants to travel at least one leg of the journey in third class, meet the truly local travelers, the poorest of our compatriots, to better understand their lives, which anyway must be exiled by economics.

I walk on board and instead of individual cabins running the length of the carriage, there are bunks pushed against each other and bags and boxes of people's belongings. There are rakes and shovels, hat boxes, and buckets filled with tools and sweaters and food. The stench is strong but more from the random buckets of food than any lack of hygiene. But one thing is clear: most of the people in third class are not here because they have such a short distance to travel—this is Siberia, there are no short distances. They are here because they lack the funds for first or second class, and even the funds to venture to the dining car for borscht or a beer, not at those prices when they can pick up some of their own at the random kiosks at the next station.

Third class travel is open; open beds and open conversations and open arguments and intimacy. There is virtually no privacy for any matter one may wish to undertake while underway. This is the price you pay for the price of third class. And it is all too familiar to me. I speak often to Michael about how much of this region of Russia, well beyond the reach of the western cities and Western culture, reminds me very much of life in St Petersburg back in the early nineties just after the coup.

Back then everything was sold for practically nothing, just so people would have money to get through the morning. I remember St. Petersburg after the coup: A woman asks if I want cigarettes, but she is not selling me a pack, just a cigarette. Another woman sells cakes and yet another books in Russian, of course. She has just two and holds one in each hand, standing silently as travelers walk by, and a few people stop and tilt their heads enough to read the title, to which she smiles and offers it to them to look at more closely, but they all refuse, at least the ones I see. I buy two cigarettes and stuff them in my pocket since I don't smoke. I would have bought a book, but I clearly do not understand enough Russian to speak let alone read a novel, and to buy it with that hanging in the air is to insult her efforts—she is not begging, she is selling. Instead I smile and nod, wishing I spoke just enough to ask of the authors.

I walk through the narrow lanes between cots in third class and remember the monastery courtyard back in the city, back then, after the fall.

Everything was for sale. A shoe, a piece of wood. Seriously, a piece of wood. What would you do? The government changed, the economy disappeared, the jobs were gone, apartments privatized which left everyone who lived in those apartments having to pay either one hundred times the normal rent or live in the streets or with five other families. The entire nation started from scratch with no instructions, little leadership, and scant resources.

One guy on the corner next to a metro stop showed up every

morning to sell empty bottles hoping someone might need an empty bottle, maybe to carry water or coffee, or for flowers since no matter how poor everyone was everyone bought flowers. Some sold old picture frames, others sold shoes, sometimes just one. Everyone sold whatever they could to whoever might have less but still needed a few items.

People sold clothes, old food, themselves. The price started high earlier in the day and dropped to nearly nothing after midnight; hell just buy her a meal and she is yours until dawn. That was Russia, St Petersburg, in post-coup nineties. Old women sold doilies or made poppy seed rolls and sold them from the corner of a bench before being chased off. The food was fresh and cheap, and these women needed the money to keep going, but still they starved, often eating the rolls to keep from dying but dying anyway. The city of old women faded fast into a city of organized crime or homelessness. The people were poor, and anything anyone could possibly want was for sale for nothing. Antique icons in their family for generations available for dollars, pennies. These women who saw what no humans should have ever witnessed were pushed to the corner of the church yard in their wheelchairs from the rooms in the now privatized hospital, and they were left there to fend for themselves.

People were starving to death, really starving to death, beneath the opulence of the high-rises and palaces. This is Russian history; whoever is not in charge has a problem with whoever is in charge. It was Nicholas's fault, Lenin's, Stalin's, Kruschev's, Brezhnev's, Gorbachev's of course, Yeltsin's most certainly, and Putin's without doubt. And many of the poor who were clearly not in charge were discharged from the cities in the west to the villages in the east, their passages paid for, third class, exiles.

So, sure, buy some cigarettes, a book. Buy another drink.

I step out onto the platform and wonder where these travelers

are heading and why. I turn back toward the next carriage and
head for the dining car, and remember the words of the math
professor, "Either you drink because you have no money, or you
drink because you're the only one that does."

Ten

Off Track

The birch trees to the north side of the tracks as we head into Irkutsk seem to have no tops. They all appear to have been cut below the lowest branch, perhaps a dozen feet above the ground, much like the trees I have seen at home after a tornado has decapitated trees at about fifteen feet high. But at home the debris is scattered about the whole forest whereas here I can see no remnants at all of the tops of the trees, as if the wind took them afar, or perhaps they were timbered, but nothing remains, I mean nothing, is left. I asked a passenger in the next booth in the dining car, but our inability to communicate forces me into a game of charades, but my motion to describe the topless birches appears more like I am threatening to cut his neck, and he quickly heads back to his cabin.

Just trying to blend Latin and Cyrillic alphabets creates a deadly collision of consonants, and I worry about the translator I have hired for the next few days, hoping he is more English savvy. None of this state of incommunicado is their fault; I am the man who is riding these tracks clear into unknown territory without so much as a phrasebook. But now we are leaving the rails for a while, trekking into the city of Irkutsk, and in particular, north of town to the great Lake Baikal.

While we are in Irkutsk we take in a museum, find some fine restaurants, and walk the waterfront of the Angara River. This is a city of almost three quarters of a million people. While a road from Moscow built in the 1700's brought the ancient outpost to life, it was actually developed in the early 1800's when the Decembrists were exiled here after the bloody uprising in St. Petersburg, and it remained the outpost for exiles and dissidents for the rest of the century and into the next. As a result, Irkutsk became the center of intellectual and social activity in Siberia when those former aristocratic rebels built beautiful wooden homes and gathered for parties and discussions of literature, opera, and politics. Most of the city burned in 1879, but when the railway came through at the turn of the century, Irkutsk was rebuilt and became known as the "Paris of Siberia." And so it is. The riverfront is home to a beautiful cathedral, a business district, and cafes carrying cuisine from throughout the world.

But that is not what attracts us to this particular stop. In fact, for those not from the region, there is just one feature which universally figures in the travel plans: Lake Baikal. It might be the number one location everyone seems to know about when you talk about Siberia. When Chekhov reached the shores of the great lake with its engulfing mystique, he wrote home that he had little desire or need to return to Moscow.

The lake is the deepest in the world and contains one fifth of all the fresh water on the planet. On a clear day you can see forty meters below the surface, it is that pure. The south edge of the lake is about forty-five miles north of the city of Irkutsk and is home to seals which do not yet know to stay away from humans. There are twenty-seven islands on the lake, which has a thirteen-hundred-mile coastline. The craziest geographical statistic of all, though, is that there are about three hundred tributaries to Lake Baikal but only one outlet, the formidable Angara River, which runs through Irkutsk, past cafes and outdoor concerts, under the Irkutsk Hydroelectric Dam as well as three other bridges to where it is joined by the Irkut River, and then it flows south another 320 miles or so to the capital of Mongolia, Ulaanbaatar.

And while the coldest month is January when the average temperature on the lake is eighteen below zero, we are here in August when it is in the mid-sixties, officially, though today it is ten degrees warmer than that despite the fog and mist coming out of the northwest.

We take a taxi to the Delta Hotel where the desk clerk informs me the guide I had hired before we arrived can come any time I wish, so I arrange for him to head over as soon as possible. His name is Alex and is from Irkutsk, he speaks English and Chinese, and he has lived in Boston and Beijing. Alex is a confident, professional, mid-twenties man who carries his cellphone like a pro and introduces us to his driver, Ivan. The four of us climb down into his small Lada and Alex tells us it will take about an hour and we definitely want to stop at a particular village along the way. We are up for anything, really, so long as we get to the lake, and so Ivan rips us out of the parking lot and out into traffic.

Alex talks to us while looking at his phone and we quickly figure out that Ivan might be out of his mind or, worse, drunk. He has this not uncommon need to look at Alex when he talks to him, and as he does the car swerves across the center line and back to the shoulder, like a scene from some bad comedy, only Ivan is a big man stuffed into the small driver's seat and my frustration increases with each turn of the head and bend in the road.

"Alex, can you please ask Ivan to keep his eyes on the road?"

He is on his phone again, and almost a minute later, Alex replies, "Oh, yes, of course! I am told he is a good driver! We have never met."

Alex says something to Ivan in Russian and the two of them laugh a bit, which is intimidating for any reason, but somehow more so when you're in the backseat, but he does keep his head forward, looks in his mirror and puts his hand up, and says, "Izvenetia. I'm sorry."

Several times on the ride up Alex insists we see this one particular small village, but I am already tainted by countless trips to St Petersburg where the guides are paid to bring a group of tourists to certain shops in the city, so I insist that since we are paying him for this and it is our time, let's just get to the lake and talk about the village after that. Both he and the driver are slightly agitated by this, but they agree.

After we park, we walk to the docks and see exactly how deep and clear the water is even at the edge. It is foggy today, and it is difficult to see very far across the water, but the lake remains calm, and peaceful, ancient, and blue, dark blue, royal blue like the color of the small guard shacks all across the country.

We stop briefly at Listvianka, a cultural area off the road on the lake, and ladies sell goods at tables in a makeshift marketplace next to the parking lot; handmade wooden bowls, spoons, cups filled with an abundance of pine nuts, touristy trinkets, and various linen and cloth items representing the heavy eastern Siberian and Mongolian influence which has occupied the area for many centuries. To that end, Alex suggests we ride the tram to Chersky Rock and pay our respects.

We are intrigued.

From a small platform we ride higher across fields of yellow and violet and rose wildflowers, all neatly manicured by a gardener already out with a weed whacker trimming along the edges of the beams and girders holding up the lines running from the lakeside booth to the top of the mountain. It is lush green, and while on the ride up we can see where we are going, which is beautiful anyway, it will be on the descent when we will take in the vista across the hills of Siberia and the reaches of the lake.

Alex, Michael, and I jump off the tram at a high point and step to the side to look back and out. "I'm so sorry it is so misty today," Alex says as we stare out, the sky indistinguishable from the lake at the horizon. I tell him it matters not, that just being up here in such silence and the muted glimmer of sun which anyway sometimes makes its way through the fog is enough to satisfy us.

"I'd be up here all the time," I say, adding, "Chekhov was right."

"He didn't want to leave," Alex adds, as if he had brought Anton up here himself. I appreciate his comment; it shows how someone who grew up here and gives tours understands the value of place, the spirit of ancestry, and the juxtaposition of such a permanent landscape with the temporal state of the visitors. Also, he reads Chekhov.

Not far from us stands a Shaman obo with pillars and ribbons. Chersky Rock is a pilgrimage site for Buddhists, the religion of the local Buryats who came to this shore in the nineteenth century. We took the lift in respect to our limited time, but pilgrims walk the rugged terrain, presumably in summer, to reach this point. They observe Shaman Buddhism, heavily practiced here, which incorporates the traditions and rituals of Buddhism, but is different and unique to Siberia and Mongolia. They clearly intersect, and the crossroads seem to be just a few feet from Chersky Rock.

Most people are more familiar with an obo made of small stones where pilgrims deposit rocks upon completion of the journey. This one is created out of ribbons of various colors, each hue representing something different in prayer. We tie one on for good luck, but once again the spirit of place takes over and I find myself saying a prayer nonetheless, albeit to a Middle Eastern deity.

We are physically, spiritually, and emotionally nowhere near the railway in a place where pilgrims have stood for centuries with a view that has not changed at all in that time. It is eternal and ever-present. My quip to Michael that we have apparently gotten off track is followed quickly by my realization that, once again, we are where we should be. We could stay, Anton and me, though apparently few ever have. Explorers came here for thousands of years yet few remained. I suppose it is the weather which keeps them at bay, but Alex reminds me that nearly all the people of Siberia were nomads, herdsmen. I stare out across the widest wilderness on Earth and hear nothing, and I cannot describe it; I will not try to describe it, the hundreds of thousands of ribbons of every color, the men who come here after war, before war, the explorers who stood here in the dead of winter, the women who come here to weep for a lost child and find some solace. They come to Chersky Rock and wait, and I have not yet found the vocabulary to communicate the experience.

Chersky is actually Ivan Czerski, a Polish man drafted into the Russian army in the 1860's assigned to a Siberian outpost. When his tour ended, he was forced to stay to account for his participation in an uprising prior to his service, so he became an explorer of his new "home." His maps were adopted by the Russian Geographical Society, and his are the most accurate of the Lake Baikal region. Not only this rock upon which we stand bears his name, but a mountain range in Kamchatka as well as other natural landmarks.

And now we are on his rock. I can hear ribbons in the breeze, and it takes on an almost eerie atmosphere as what seems like the spirits of previous travelers' scatter about us, urge us on, call us to stay a while longer. But we must return to the lake and then to Irkutsk, and then eastward on the railway. We are on a journey, after all. I watch ribbons flutter in the breeze and wonder about all the journeys of previous pilgrims, for centuries even, and their passing through here. Am I merely rehashing the traditional journey theme? If so, I would be in good company with the likes of Homer and Cervantes, as well as the sea of writers who attempt and fall short, which is where I find myself today. Standing here on this rock overlooking the vast Lake Baikal I wonder if on this particular journey the protagonist is the rock and the lake and the odd topless trees; and the dynamic moment which so endears the reader is when people *don't* come, or at the very least they certainly do not stay, and this wilderness is left to be as it should. We are static characters, humanity, nameless, in this wilderness. I want to defy Odysseus and Quixote and insist that the only way at all to understand the journey is to step off of it for a moment and see it from up high, where we have an unobstructed view, where even the Shaman sits and waits.

On the way back to the city we stop at the village Alex insisted we visit, and he is, of course, right. It is a recreated tourist area representing the peoples of Siberia through the ages, how they lived, how their houses were set up, as well as their places of worship and schools. We enjoy each structure more than the previous one, and there is much to see, but I am taken up short by a large yurt on the grounds, built by Mongolians who work inside and explain the story of their people, serve tea, and sell small goods. We have a milky Mongolian tea and imagine life here, quietly passing the time closer to God than anywhere I have been. Make no mistake, this is sacred ground for what is not present, no shops, no hotels, no tacky tourist traps with t-shirts and bottles of coke. It is as it has been since it first came to be, and we are made to understand we are just two more on that track as time ticks ahead of us.

American writer Robert Miltner wrote there is a "human need to lineate, to initiate a binary division against the natural impulses of geography." The tracks go into and out from a tunnel, side by side. Moving into the future in the direction you face is not difficult; staying on track is not a struggle for most—just keep going. But up here in the mountains above the deepest lake in the world, formed billions of years ago from glaciers long gone, the Shaman suggestions which settle strongest with me are the ones insisting life exists off the tracks, and that the ride was never intended to solely reach some destination, be it Vladivostok or old age, but intended instead as a transport from one part of life to the next. Since departing St. Petersburg on a ride barreling east, I have learned to focus on what it is like to let someone else control the engine while I mix with the multitudes in a string of individual moments, each one static and beautiful and present, but collectively a fluid stream of lives. Out here, unreachable by Moscow time, it is easy to lose track, and just as simple to forget what we were chasing down those tracks to begin with, and I finally discover that I do not need to keep going after all. Moments like this are why I write.

I step out of the yurt and walk toward the car where the others wait when I see to the west the topless birches which we rolled past on our way from Yekaterinburg. I walk to the car and ask Alex, "Do you know why those trees have no tops?" He looks at them for a moment and says, "No, I don't. But I will find out and tell you the next time you come to the lake to better understand it." He seems prophetic, and it leaves me with a sense of hope. I find something metaphoric in trees with no tops, and I want to say so, to laugh and propose they are leftover trees from the days of Stalin, that perhaps he didn't want those exiled here to be able to climb to high or see too far. But all of this seems too complicated for the narrow grey space Alex and I share in our Venn graph of languages. Instead I say, "I really love birches," and he nods, and I realize he must think I am desperately simple-minded.

We head down the highway for the Delta Hotel, Ivan not talking, when Alex turns around and apologizes. "I hope you do not think me rude, Bob," he says. "I use cell phone to translate all you say and what I wish to say in reply." I did think he was being rude. I just should have asked. I keep forgetting St. Bernard, who said, "We need to learn to make excuses for other people." I hope others make excuses for me.

Eleven

Impressionism

Among the reasons my son has joined me on this journey is his profession; as a photographer he came to capture what he could of this country. So we watch, the two of us, separated by both a generation and a genre. He was born just as Russia was no longer the Soviet Union, and I was raised during the Cold War. He observes from as many angles as possible, trying always to create a whole picture from various perspectives, as might a cubist. I dissect, writing my way through the questions in some attempt to separate the truth from the not so true. I find writing to be a more investigative method of unearthing the illusions around us. Yet it is difficult to deny that photography exposes, quite literally, life as it happens.

I have a photograph in my office of four women on a bench in Russia. They are all old, clearly survivors of the siege in the "city of old women." It is black and white taken by Valentine, a Russian friend who makes wooden bowls and wins awards with his camera. When we first arrived in St Petersburg we went right to the market and found my old friend. He was drunk, as usual, and surrounded by tourists wanting some of his works. He ignored them to talk to us, and he and Michael did the best they could to talk about their shared craft, Michael trying the entire time to negotiate a deal for one of Valentine's uniquely Russian cameras.

In the photograph at home, the women wear kerchiefs and look the complete image of what we in the west might call "Babushkas." In Russian it means Grandma; to us, any old woman wearing something on her head. When people see the picture, they usually say, "Oh, how Russian!"

That is true. But really, it is what Valentine wanted it to be. I have a picture a friend shot in a graveyard on the south side of the city. It is of an old woman lying down on the bench. The image is clear; it is a sunny day, there are other mourners walking about and from the picture alone, she seems to be sleeping, or drunk. Actually, she was crying for her husband and son who died during the siege and whom in the early 1940's she herself carried to the mass grave just feet from her. When I spoke to her, she had been clasping a picture of the two—strong man and tender young child, father and son forever immortalized in a photo which, for this woman, collapses time and love and memory. The contrast is debilitating. Just meters away are their remains; just decades away are the moments she'll remember most when she turned over the sleigh she used to haul them here. No one took a picture then. No picture then would capture the grief, the fear, but also the resolution to keep going.

Writing has always preserved the thoughts of humanity, the turmoil, and the struggles. But my son's art form, and that of Valentine, slaps down life's reality in images of such blatant truths that a thousand times a thousand words would not come close to such honesty. During the siege, some photographers took pictures in the city besieged for nine hundred days by the Nazis. One is of a woman standing in the snow and at her feet is a body covered in a blanket; a relative, perhaps, though it could also be just another victim of starvation or disease, left in the street by family, or living in the street due to the bombing, and the standing woman might have merely been passing by on her way to find water beneath the frozen Neva River. Pictures of that scene are everywhere. It is tragic, of course, but it is history.

We stare at the image because we realize the brutal actuality of it, but we want to forget it at the same time.

Shortly after Parisian Joseph Niepce developed the first photograph of architecture in the 1820's, it faded like a distant memory, a latent recollection of some smile, some quick glance. But Louis Daguerre bathed the image in salt and less than two hundred years later we have something to hang on the wall. It was that simple. No magic, no soul-stealing, no tube paints, or art school; just chemicals and light. In India, a myth remained for a long time that having a photograph taken would shorten one's life expectancy. In parts of East Asia some believe taking an image of an odd number of people is bad luck. In Russia, photography is as much a part of their cultural presence as smoked salmon and balalaika music.

The world has traveled quite the distance to get to the digital moments we capture now. We worked through exposure time, wet plates, dry plates, several journeys of gains and sacrifices. Early problems included finding the right developing solutions, then it was making multiple prints, then improving quality of detail. But in the end, they kept moving forward through the Calotype process, the small box Kodak, to the myriad possibilities today. And all photographers through the years have had a common ambition—they long for the defining shot.

Valentine's table in the marketplace is covered with hundreds of varying pictures, most pasted to the ripped off covers of old books, some just black and white prints, and all of them disturbingly human, like the four women on the bench. I have watched Michael shoot pictures of people on the platforms and reflections in the passing canals. He will push his way through a half dozen memory cards of thousands of photos in an effort to find a few he can salvage, hold up, and say, "This, this is what it was like." Photographers and writers share that struggle to communicate with precision; images, like words, can often remain vague.

I have shoe boxes filled with photographs stored beneath beds and in drawers, photo albums in the back of top shelves of closets and in file cabinets, including thousands of photographs of my twenty-something trips to Russia. The value is apparent: St Petersburg will never again be what it was in the early nineties—a place still dark and absent of western influence but heavy in Russian traditions. The streets when I first went were absent of billboards and neon. There were virtually no advertisements, and the cars were nearly all the same, small four door Ladas.

I have a video from 1994 taken on the metro during rush hour. Everyone is still and no one is talking, and the train was sitting still. After fifteen seconds, you can hear my voice and a man's head turns and looks toward me—without that, it might have been a silent film; even a photograph. Today, the streets resemble Times Square with enough advertising to keep the city's electricity bureau alive and well. The metro is swimming in activity, music, and the hustle of a city more akin to London.

Images can define an identity. A colleague took photos of the city and showed them to my classes in America. He showed the old people in the dumpsters, the homeless begging in the monastery graveyard, the injured Chechnya War vet leaning against a wall on Nevsky Prospect searching for money. I asked why he didn't show the spires from the early nineties before there were crosses, and then again after the crosses were returned. Why didn't he show the majesty of the Hermitage and the Smolney Cathedral? I know he took those images; I have seen them. But he did what all photographers do, whether for a newspaper or a class—he defined, with his own impression, what he wanted us to see. I would have preferred photographs which exposed the simplicity of then, the experience of then. Maybe all of the photographs combined might initiate a sense of interest and experience, their sum enabling others in the west to calculate the city's political path from Gorbechev to Putin, but there will always be gaps, some dark ages.

There will also always be the pursuit of one picture that eliminates the need for volumes on the subject. This "one shot" attempt at capturing identity is tragically common. Lenin's waxy body encased forever in Red Square; Stalin at the summit, an old Tolstoy sitting alone in some garden. The rest of the world, too, has succeeded in finding the right images: Marilyn Monroe on the grate; a student in front of a tank at Tiananmen Square; the Space Shuttle Challenger explosion against a cobalt blue sky; the towers tumbling; the napalm girl; the wall coming down.

It's the darkroom's equivalent of the sound bite. Photojournalists spend their lives looking for The Image—the shot no one will ever forget. But what we so easily overlook is the depth of humanity beyond the Kodachrome. Martin at the Lincoln Memorial; some hippy putting a flower in the gun; Hiroshima's mushroom cloud; Jack Kennedy in Dallas. None of these expose the struggle, the innocence, the inhumanity. The "soldiers lifting the flag at Iwo Jima" seems victorious, doesn't it? But what's over the hill, out on the fields that we cannot see? The shots of the Winter Palace do not come with history lessons, the Czars reign, the Bolshevik's march. A glance at a portrait of Catherine the Great does not reveal her German roots, her insight, or the lessons she learned through correspondence with Voltaire. Pictures lie and manipulate. The Smolney Cathedral, blue and white, rises stark against the Russian sky, the onion domes spinning prayers to God, but it was from one of the domes that Seraphim fell and landed softly, running off toward canonization. Most people see the skyline; I see miracles, but then I have more information than the common viewer. This is a shared problem with writing. Those who have tramped across Siberia will visualize my words with more accuracy than those who read from their front porch in Virginia. So like the photographer I must choose the correct angle, manipulate what passages I need to illuminate and which ones to leave grey, slightly short of comprehension.

An image of troops crossing a trench in the ice and snow shows movement despite its perpetual stillness. Because of the photo, on the steppe the war rages on. In Leningrad one photograph explores without mercy emaciated children, hours from death. Women dig holes in the frozen Neva and around them the remains of an explosion fill the frame.

What is the siege to a photographer? How does one explore the statistics and horror or death by starvation and disease while snapping a picture with the right aperture? There are photographs and newsreels of the siege, but while contemplating the photographers who captured the carnage and fatality of those years, it is difficult not to wonder where the line between voyeur and participant exists. In a review of the modern-day silent film *Blockade*, Jana Prikryl notes that "Images turn out to be slippery things. During the course of the film, Leningraders ladle melt-water from fissures in ice coating the streets; they put out fires; they wrench wooden boards (presumably for fuel) from a stadium dominated by a poster of Stalin; they stumble along snowbound boulevards, picking their way around abandoned corpses, pulling sleds that hold buckets of provisions, or bulging parcels or tightly-wrapped bodies. Several nightmarish shots of the dead (and their weeping relatives) punctuate an otherwise sedate record of survival. One even gets the feeling that Leningrad was a hive of subdued activity during the Siege: the streets (at least the ones that were filmed) appear well-trodden and people courteously help each other clamber over cottage-sized drifts of snow. You want to ask where they are all going. Why is that woman smiling into the camera?" Seeing reels of the siege, witnessing the sorrow in the faces and cries of veterans and old women, emphasizes how pointless and monstrous it seems. How did she manage to survive? How did he find wood for a fire? Can they taste the sawdust mixed in the bread dough? How did he get that scar on his forehead?

Really, there are no words because of the images.

The Victory Day posters in the west mostly show just that, Victory. It is "The Kiss," it is the parades and celebrations from London to Paris to New York. There are soldiers returning home and they are wearing white. The world was starting over, once again virgin. The allies were victorious because they won, they pushed back the troops; they forced fascists to the table to sign the surrender papers.

And so it was in Leningrad, starting over, but the images are different. Allied troops deliver food, onions and potatoes, across the frozen Lake Ladoga. Women walk the streets looking for water and food, and the closest a viewer comes to recognizing "victory" is the lack of fear on her face, replaced solely with a sense of relief. Relief, after all, is a victory in itself. The victory came in not dying; the extraordinary achievement of the survivors of the siege was in defeating the outrageous odds. The irony of Leningrad is that for nine hundred days, the shock of war kept most from crying; they buried bodies without speaking, a stoic response from anyone nearby. Part of it was shock, part of it was dehydration, and part of it was the numbness of persistent and repetitive death. But all of it crashed through the emotional levies when the blockade broke and people flooded the streets crying in joy, in relief. These photographs exist, but they lack contrast. True images of Leningrad during the blockade must include both fear and courage, anger and forgiveness, mourning and acceptance.

A simple example of visual deception: That woman on the bench, bent over, seemingly asleep, dirty, smelly, unmoving despite the other two people sitting on the same bench—she appears drunk and disturbed. The picture passed among colleagues and they all agreed to her callousness at sleeping on a bench in such a sacred place as the graveyard on Victory Day. Then I tell them about her husband and son, just feet away, and the black and white photograph of the two, smiling. Suddenly some feel shame at their assumptions. Photographs and writing share this as well, this deception, allowing us to make assumptions of other people instead of excuses *for* other people.

So no photograph carries a clear image. And rarely does one take pictures of the most defining moments; the solider coming through the door to announce freedom; the sitting down to a warm meal with the few remaining survivors; the coming and going after nearly three years of hiding. Those moments are clear to veterans and survivors alike, and will, most likely, be the defining memory for them. That cannot be translated to shutter speed and developing fluids. The best photograph of the worst moments only scratches the surface of what really remains indelible to them.

The essence of any war on film, but particularly one as personal and brutal as the siege of a city, is problematic. The real image has imperfections. The scars of a soldier imply injury and loss, when those scars may be the result of a great and indefinable victory, either on the battlefield or by delivering food through enemy troops or across a frozen lake in sub-zero, arctic conditions. Those scars are part of history, slices of the current events when the photo was taken. They are about survival and perseverance. Still, these multiple images, these mirrored events, remain allusive to the lens.

In the history books we see photos of Stalin and Churchill and Roosevelt; we see the Nazis surrounding and saluting Hitler. These are front page photos, above the fold, caption and credit. It is the war-equivalent of taking pictures of the Winter Palace, the great Cathedrals, and the Peter and Paul Fortress spire which stands above the rest of the city, and then showing them as slides of "what St Petersburg is like." But that's not Russia, that is not even close.

Russia is the woman in the Hermitage watching the Rembrandts, making sure no one uses a flash, and everyone has a ticket for their cameras. She survived the siege, she lost family, she moved on. Russia is the soup—fish soup, beet soup, cabbage soup, and the tea from a samovar after dinner. It is Easter cake, it is pocket icons, it is the rustling of something unknown in the grass next to caved in caskets and entombed saints.

Russia is the bow to the knees in genuflection; it is the difference between the con artist selling fake icons and the man trying to sell ancient icons to feed his family. The city is the dank, horrific way of life for a teenage girl with no sense of hope and the young man with few career choices if he wants to make any money at all. This cannot be photographed.

A life cannot be chiseled to the proverbial thousand words. We can try and digitally close the decades, slam together centuries with just the right F-stop and angle of light. We can do that; we can collapse time keeping our fathers young, our grandfathers alive, ourselves something more than a myth for posterity.

Yet the exclusion of flesh and bone–and I suppose, in some small way, soul–makes capturing someone's essence a nearly impossible task. Add to that the horror and inhumane conditions of war, of pestilence and starvation, and the true images get left behind.

George Eastman wrapped up some flexible film in 1884 and a few decades later the family of Czar Nicholas II became the most famous photographed royal family of their day. It was, in fact, the lure of a photograph to convince the world they were fine and that the Bolsheviks had treated them well that brought the family to be massacred in the basement of a palace. The pictures of Nicholas and Alexandra and their kids might define Czarist Russia more than any other images. The photo of Nicholas and his son Alexi which Michael bought for me at the shrine is forever a father and son, though for me it is also a mirror reflecting a fluid image between a fallen Czar and the prince, and a hopeful writer and a young photographer.

Truth be told, no picture is permanent. They fade as we do; they resolve themselves into the salt of the earth. Real images are allusive except in how we recall them. Michael holds his camera against a clear spot on the glass and tries to get a good image of a graveyard we pass at dawn. It can be a good shot and he knows it; even I can see that when we pass, and I ask him, "Did you get it?"

"I'm not sure, maybe?"

"Did you take more than one? It might help if you took a bunch."

He smiles. "I took about eighty." Now I feel stupid, but that is good; he is a pro. I think of Valentine's table piled high with images. Look at his image of the long carriage hallway, empty save one Russian man at the far end looking back. I have a story about that guy if you want to know more. Photographs are doors into narratives, isolating one point but encapsulating an entire story, sometimes a life. Look at the picture of the old woman selling cucumbers; I am moved every time I see her standing there, perfectly still. Note my son's image of the wheeltapper bending under the carriage listening to the tone of the iron as he bangs it with a crowbar; his story is ancient.

"I took about eighty," he says casually, as if he meant to say, "only eighty." But then I think of my file cabinets stuffed with repetitive rough drafts. I think of my journals and writings right here in the dining car, spread out and piled high, trying to say one particular thing about the provodnitsa, the attendant, but not quite sure I have gotten it right, so I keep writing. I just keep writing.

Photo Gallery

Familiar markings of the TSRR carriages.

One of the first locomotives on the TSRR.

Nicholas and Alexi with Alexandra on Imperial train, St Petersburg to Yekaterinberg.

Church on the Blood in Honor of All Saints Resplendent in the Russian Land.

Entrance to one of the stations

Hallway in the carriage with cabins on the left.

In the passage between cars.

At the bar in the
Dining Car.

Countryside east of Irkutsk.

Old and new Irkutsk.

Farmhands in Eastern Siberia.

At one of the stations.

Michael in the passageway
with his harmonica.

Platform in Siberia on a warm August afternoon.

Loading the linens.

Man selling to villagers from the back of his Lada.

Rail workers on a break.

One of many signs instructing travelers what NOT to do. (left) Women from the local villages sell their homemade goods. (right)

Station worker telling the engineer to stop.

Village woman selling homemade food at a station.

A father and son waiting for the train.

A late night early morning stop.

A standard guard shack at a crossing in eastern Siberia.

Birch Trees.

Bob with translator, Alex, heading to the tram at Lake Baikal.

Bob with his translator Alex at Chersky Rock.

Alexander Ivanovich with Bob.

Michael hiking
high above
Lake Baikal.

Entering the flood zone along the Russian-China border.

Michael and
one of the Chess
Gang of Four.

Michael with a few chessmates.

Michael
against the
Russian
Chess Gang.

An abandoned old mission across the border near the Amur River.

A small village in the east.

The cucumber lady.

The dining car.

A Veteran of the
Great Patriotic War.

Finally! At the Vladivostok Train Station.

Twelve

Philosophy

We're back on board, barreling ahead. I derailed my life for this journey across European and Asian Russia. At home, at work, the gives and takes of keeping at it to keep life going makes it difficult to slow down enough to think about what direction I am heading. We, all of us, roll along often mindlessly, usually without much introspection or self-analysis. But here, cruising forward into the unknown, finally enables me to stop, step aside, and study my life, because no matter where I am, even when I'm standing still—sometimes especially when I'm standing still—"what's next" is right around the bend, just past the next station.

Some say a train ride can be monotonous, even boring, to pass the same landscape, walk down the same thin, hot hallway, sleep in the same claustrophobic cot day and night, but I wonder how that differs from an American's normal routine driving to work, walking through the corridors of the office building, going home to the same television shows and sleeping in the same bed. The value of our routine is tied to how we enjoy the time we spend, not simply where we are going and how we will get there. Here, how we experience an endless sea of pastoral views is dependent on the angle of the sun, the sound of the train, the people laughing in the dining car, and conversation with a companion, of course. But sometimes it is also the silence, the deep baritone silence of late night when you glimpse a soft light in a guardhouse window and know some soul whose job it is to mark the time of your passing is inside reading. In some deep butterfly-effect way, he serves his purpose on my pilgrimage, as did the woman in London who processed the train tickets, and the blueberry-selling babushka, and the writer at a party in Virginia ten years ago who said I had to see Siberia. Still, despite my meticulous planning, what happens now is out of my control, and there are times when it is not unusual to look blankly out at the landscape in the fading moonlight. Sometimes my mind is quiet, safe within the mere *dream* of coming here, which for some people is enough, but which employs no one, such as the hotel clerk in St. Petersburg who made sure we left for the station on time, or my friend Igor Chertok who recommended hotels across the nation, or my father, who promised to hold out long enough for us to come back and tell him our story, or my son, who gathered up his forces and followed me on board.

And now we are back on the moving train for the longest stretch, all the way to Vladivostok. We quickly get settled and head to our familiar zone between cars.

"City of New Orleans," Michael says and stares out at the platform watching others board.

"No."

"It's a classic train song!"

"Too easy. Too obvious!"

"Okay then, 'Waiting for a Train' by Jimmie Rogers."

I nod my head, "Wow, that's a good one. Damn."

Michael counts down, "Nine... eight... seven..."

"Um..."

"Six... five... four..."

"Wabash Cannonball!"

"You made that up!"

"I did not! Turn of the century. Turn of *my* century, not yours. I think the Carter Family did it in the 1920's."

Michael nods and walks toward the door. "I'm hungry."

Indeed, we are moving, again. It is late in the day and both of us are exhausted from exploring Irkutsk and Lake Baikal, spending time in an old Scottish pub in the city and walking endless miles along the Angara River. My heart rate increased when we passed back through the terminal to board, bags in tow, feeling old hands at Russian transport, and mentally changing back to Moscow time thirty-three-hundred miles from Moscow. E.M. Forester wrote that we pass through terminal gates to the "glorious and unknown." Yes. We board remembering that anything is possible on a train. As fellow travel writer Paul Theroux points out, "A great meal, a binge, a visit from card players, an intrigue, a good night's sleep, and strangers' monologues framed like Russian short stories." Anything.

Joseph Brodsky wrote he would prefer the country he could leave to the country he could not. He was being literal, but like all vague ideas by dead writers and revolutionaries, I prefer to push the metaphoric envelope. For some, the most impenetrable bars are those which imprison hearts and souls, and we move through our own lives as exiles always searching for some semblance of home, of security. Certainly, there is comfort and peace in predictability. A person can be in a cave and find hope while his brother is in a caravan of pilgrims destined for some sacred spot and never discover a moment of grace.

I will never be able to recall all I've experienced on this ride, so I let markers trigger my memory, such as the smell of onions which brings me outside on the platforms where ladies hold trays of pastries and meat pies. Or the smell of vodka which brings me to Alexander Ivanovich, stretched out on his bunk next to mine, his scarred and calloused feet resting on a pillow, suggesting his laborious life. Or how hearing "This Land is Your Land" will never again bring me to the American West but instead the Siberian hills. But pieces of my memory will need to be sacrificed on this journey of ours, and it calls to mind my father's stories of his youth, or of his young-adult years riding the Long Island Railway from the Island to the city, and a distant vagueness accompanied so many of those tales as we moved toward my own adulthood. I used to pride myself in my power of recall for even the most minute details, but now I've accepted a new reality: this train, despite the strongest efforts of all those who've ridden before, is moving on. A certain aphasia exists but instead of the words being just beyond reach, it is the visceral, the sensorial memory which will fade and return, fade and return. Sometimes I will smell the fry cakes sold at the stations and I will be able to summon their taste as certain as if I brought one home for such a moment. Other times, already, since our departure out of St. Petersburg seems like months ago in these short weeks, I will think of the meal in the dining car of smoked salmon and sliced cucumbers and wonder if it was all something I read about, or one of Michael's pictures he showed me one afternoon. Such is the nature of travel in retrospect.

Add to that the abyss of communication we have tried to leap during this crossing. It is sometimes terrifying to travel where language can feel fraudulent, and hopes can seem slanderous. "Taking a new step, uttering a new word, is what people fear most," wrote Dostoevsky. Well, yes, of course. But he added that it takes something more than intelligence to act intelligently. This is not an intellectual exercise alone, moving along like this. Instinct is involved and a tremendous amount of observation. But in the end, it seems that the advice provided by generations of exiles is once again accurate: there is no generic journey; each one is unique and must be followed by the nature of each traveler. That should cover both the literal and the metaphorical.

I can find plenty of quotes to fill these pages, from Tolstoy to Jack Reed to our own cabin mates, but Nabokov remains most relative when attempting to capture life in motion: "Words without experience are meaningless." Rewrite: Words without memories are ghosts, shadows.

For now, I can smell the borscht drifting out of the kitchen and the attendant gives me a smile. It is late and we head farther east, and further east still.

Thirteen

Wheeltappers

This is the story of the wheeltapper.

I stand on the station platform about three a.m., not sure of where we are and not positive how long it will be before we move on, probably the normal twenty minutes or so. When the train stops for more than ten minutes at one of the many stations, the doors open and the steps go down so passengers who so wish can disembark and stretch their legs, maybe grab a bite to eat from the ladies selling baked goods and warm pastries filled with meat and onions; though it is rare to find vendors at this hour. The night air is chilly but a welcome break from the warm cabins on the train.

Men in coveralls walk along the tracks on the gravel, one hand on the bottom of the train for balance, and the other hand holding a short, metal, hammer-like rod. The workers are called wheeltappers, and as they walk, they reach under the train and tap the wheels checking for the sound; a cracked wheel sounds different than a solid one, and after long runs along wilderness track, it might not be unusual for something to have gone wrong.

Like the time in 2008 when an Aeroflot plane crashed near Perm in the Urals, killing eighty-eight people on board, though none on the ground. But plane debris on the tracks damaged wheels on some of the carriages forcing a rerouting of the train, which complicated the smallest of plans for passengers.

And in 1989, a gas pipeline running alongside the tracks not far from Moscow exploded just as two trains were passing each other, and the ball of fire incinerated hundreds of passengers— businessmen, women, children, who moments earlier might have been looking out the same windows as ours, drinking tea, laughing. That is how tragedy works; it follows a moment of laughter.

And in 2019, four carriages completely jumped the tracks about fifty miles from the Kuenga Station in eastern Siberia. No one on board was injured, and the accident occurred in a relatively safe area because of proximity to assistance, but there are sections of this journey, particularly along the Amur and down in the taiga region, which can be dangerous. Passengers in the Kuenga accident were only delayed about six hours in all and then were on their way since the larger stations in the middle of the line, from Novosibirsk, through Ulan-Ude, and points east, allowed for crews with cranes to correct the derailed carriages quite quickly. The reports make it all sound programmed and safe; but change the time of day and move the accident to the southeast, or on the line circling Lake Baikal, and tragedy has a sharper edge.

Some insist all derailments can be avoided with the new technology which detects damage to the wheels, eliminating human error from the inspections. In fact, most railways have replaced the wheeltappers with these automated methods to ensure the integrity of the wheels as well as the axle boxes, which the wheeltappers touch with their hands to see if they have overheated, but the Siberian railway all the way to Vladivostok still employs these men. They rest briefly in the station between runs day and night, and then they are bent under the cars and tap the metal to listen for the awkward clank of a crack.

When the train stops like this in each station, the bathrooms on board are locked so no one will use them. To flush the commode, one steps on a foot-pedal device which opens the bottom, and the contents dump right onto the tracks as we roll speedily along. Most of the reach is wilderness, so the compost is not normally noticed. But the workers at a station do not want someone going to the bathroom and then stepping on the metal release and dropping their excrement onto the tracks next to people waiting, or, worse, onto the back of a wheeltapper. But this also means that about ten minutes before approaching a station, particularly one where a lengthy stop is planned, a line forms at the onboard bathrooms.

Some stations have small stores, kiosks mostly, though a few of the larger stations might have walk-in stores, all of which carry assorted beverages, foods, soaps, personal items, electronics, magazines, and cigarettes. They remind me of the small kiosks in subways in New York. When it is time to re-board, the women who monitor each car might call quietly to the surrounding area and wait a moment before pulling the stairs up and locking the door, but if a passenger is in a store or otherwise doesn't make it back in the time scheduled for the stop (and it is almost always on time), the passenger simply misses the train and has to buy a new ticket for the next one which comes along. It is why so many do not disembark to begin with; that and most passengers just want to sleep and get where they are going with little interruption. There is a chart in each carriage with the names and length of each stop. Generally, the stairs do not go down to the platform for the stations at which we stop for less than ten minutes. When they do, however, I head outside. We are in this for the long-haul and to experience the journey, so I like to walk around the platform, get fresh air and take in the atmosphere, such as in larger stations which are always active; places like Novosibirsk, Omsk, Irkutsk, and others whose populations can reach well into hundreds of thousands of inhabitants, not including summer residents and the occasional tourists. These warmer months turn the lower reaches of Siberia into an inexpensive and beautiful locale. Still, the vast majority of stations on this six-thousand-mile journey are little more than platforms in the middle of nowhere with one guard. If we have stopped at those, I have slept through the experience.

Another benefit to these brief respites at various stations is the old women who wander here from the nearby village or farms. They carry trays of food to sell to the passengers, and their prices are criminally low. This is, after all, extremely rural Russia where one's income is based solely upon one's needs. There's the lady selling her blueberries, and another holding bags of dried fish, and another with a tray of what can best be described as homemade hot pockets, flaky and hot, and should I ride this way again, I'd take all my meals on the station platforms where life is stripped down to its essentials, and the women bare their way of life as proof of fate, a sentence of sorts, and they carry their trays without complaint or worry, talking to each other about the day, the weather, the normal local conversations taking place like this around the world, and they sell their fruit, their flat bread covered in locally-made cheese and tomatoes—Russian pizza really— which Michael bought from two young girls across a fence a few stations back. I bought pirogies from an old woman who dumped a few dozen in a baggie for about fifty cents. But at this hour and for such a short stop, no one is selling food and I stand at the end of the platform and stare north, "Out across frigging Siberia," I say to myself, and am more awake than seems possible, staring out into a blanket of stars despite the flood of light from the station, and my "awakeness" turns into a sort of clarity, and I think, *this is why I'm here. This is why I came.*

At one station yesterday, a wheeltapper banged away at the wheel and put his hand on the axle box as usual, and all was fine. But I wondered what would happen if it sounded cracked or the box was overheated. How long would it take for them to determine everything is fine and we can continue? Or, if it so happens, how long before a new train replaces the broken one? I find the wheeltappers conspicuously redundant; not because of the technology which has pushed them to the edge of their usefulness, but because if they did hear a sound which resonated as something broken, or they in fact burned their hand on an overheated box, I am not convinced they would do anything more than mark it in a report and send us on our way. It is best not to think about it, or, like my son, simply stay inside and sleep during these shorter stops. Still, the vast numbers of travelers in this world remain oblivious to the possible dangers beneath their feet. It is the same in flight, on buses, rental cars. One of the most significant aspects of travel, particularly on foreign soil with little common ground and few cultural connections, is the necessary trust in everyone to do their job. The trans-Siberian railway is a tough balance of remaining slightly suspicious and paranoid, while being mostly trusting and at ease. It is a leap of faith. I found myself listening near one of the wheeltappers a few nights ago and even though I knew I wouldn't know a cracked sound from a good one without comparison, I quickly retreated in fear I actually would somehow recognize a disturbance in the metal and then board the train waiting for a derailment. I'd rather not know, I suppose.

Still, sometimes sleep does not come easy out here. The nature of moving through wilderness for hours on end without steady conversation means a wandering mind, at least for me. These days I think about my father and the time we spent together, clearly because of this time I have with my son. My dad was a busy man, but when he was home, he was completely home; no one called from work, no one distracted him beyond the sports announcers on television, which anyway we watched together with my brother. Mostly, though, I think about how much I have learned about being a father from him, yet it took me twenty years to understand the lessons, and they come too late to tell him. Dad and I communicated fine without words and despite our generational differences; I knew how much he loved us all, I knew when we had his attention and when we did not, and I knew what piqued his interest, all through observation and practice. It turns out that humans reveal their emotions, desires, and dislikes the same everywhere. Language comes in multiple forms.

I look at my rail companions out in the cool, night air. It is often difficult to tell the difference between exiles and travelers; we are all forced away from home for various reasons, from political dissidence to restless imagination. Here in Siberia, the Yenets, the Nenets, the Huns, the Scythians, the Yakuts, and others all had part in defining Siberia; the Cossacks perhaps most famously. A Mercator map of 1595 marks a Fort Siber and the surrounding lands as Siber, and it is said to be the origin of Siberia, which occupies seventy percent of all of Russia. Interestingly, the first mention of "Siber" is from Chinese travelers in the thirteenth century and so the word origin is likely Chinese, possibly meaning "Western Borderland." The first mention of the territory in the west, however, is from the fourteenth century on a Catalan Map, which names this area "Sebur" along with all the lands east of the Volga.

Really, who knows? Documents are vague, each invader and explorer claiming a new origin story. For me, it is the vast stretch of deeply beautiful forest and steppe I came here to cross with my twenty-year-old son. Trotsky passed through here, and Dostoevsky, Solzhenitsyn, Shalamov, and Avvakum the Archpriest, who made the first eyewitness account of the territory and the people. Famously, Peter the Great briefly exiled his son Alexi here for trying to overthrow the government. Not all fathers and sons get along.

But if we did decide to stay, probably no one would notice.

Siberia is so vast only three people reside per square kilometer. Thirty million people live here, and nearly all of them reside along the rails. Yes, it gets cold and dreary, but the summers are warm with temperatures averaging in the 60s and 70s, and the vegetation abundant.

As much as I am outside like this when we stop or when I'm staring out through the plate-glass windows, I'm just as often inside on some internal pilgrimage. To be certain, we cannot journey anywhere unless we are also willing to travel within and explore our souls, discover those remote areas inside we have long ago locked behind our own gulag gates. It is tragic that it often takes a trip elsewhere for most people to explore themselves, excavate their lives and question where they are, where they are going; tap on one's own soul and see if it still sounds right. I am always grateful for this "inscape" as Thomas Merton called it.

Inevitably, a few other passengers venture out to smoke or just cool off. They gather along the unused tracks and talk about the distance home or the work they had been doing, and I cautiously walk to the end of the tracks to gaze north into the forests or the seemingly endless steppe and wonder what world I am now on so far from the cafes of the east coast of the United States. These people who live here are not exiles; they live here, grew up here, and most likely are descendants of someone exiled at least a generation or two ago, but are here by choice nonetheless, because it is all they know, their family and friends, their job, their memories, their afternoon walks home from school, their hunting and fishing stories, their history, and their unrestricted ambitions here so far from the long reach of Moscow. And me, passing through, like so many writers before passed through; what good are my stories after so many other stories by those writers I read in preparation? Will my work be redundant? I laugh to myself. *Maybe this is the reason no one writes about Siberia*, I think. So I stand on the edge of the rail thinking one should probably actually live here to write about it, but one could only live here if one was from here; yes, there are places like that throughout the world, including rural Virginia, places where to live there is only possible if one's roots ran deeper than a generation or two. The only alternative for nomads like me, then, is to pass through, like the pilgrim in Kozlov's narrative, without any need to be anywhere except in prayer, and always just a day away from where I am going.

When the woman on the platform indicates it is time to return to the train, to our cabins, I do so quietly, pausing briefly to glance at the wheels. I wonder if the dirt on the metal is, in fact, dirt, or a crack missed by the tapper. Inside, I open the thick cabin door and note our cabin mates and Michael still fast asleep, and I climb into my bunk, tap on my book light so as not to wake Michael or anyone else, and I write in my journal and try to recall the works of previous writers who traveled this way. Before leaving, I collected enough literature about Siberia to fill a bookcase. About the people, the far stretches of the furthest corners of this grand and mysterious and infinitely present landscape. The work which comes to mind immediately, of course, is Anton Chekhov's *A Journey to the End of the Russian Empire*; the one book I actually did bring. But equally present in my insomnia-prone mind is Ian Frazier's *Travels in Siberia* and *The Long Walk* by Slavomir Rawicz, whose chilling account of escape from a gulag followed by a treacherous walk to India is inspiring and gut-wrenching for its descriptions of the reality that was the prison system in the Soviet Union in which countless souls perished. Of course I read Colin Thubron's trilogy simply because everyone asks if I read them when I said I was headed to Siberia. Personally, it was Chekhov who came closest to my motivation and emotional pull, with a little of Frazier's humorous perspective.

Dostoevsky's *House of the Dead*, John Valliant's *The Tiger* which soon enough would become all too real, and Anna Reid's

The Shaman's Coat set a tone in my mind which turned out to be quite accurate—the land to the east is difficult to isolate into a particular "period"; it is ancient and cutting-edge, it is political and innocent, it is a dangerous destination and a peaceful escape, and one can understand the mix more accurately after reading those works. And, certainly, Bob Shacochis' essay, "Here the Bear and the Mafia Roam," since Bob was a primary motivator for heading here to begin with.

Solzhenitsyn and Tolstoy too, whose *War and Peace* begins with the Napoleonic invasion of Russia but culminates with the Decembrist's movement, and so too I read books about the Decembrist's exile in Irkutsk, one of the most advanced and exciting cities in Russia. But the one work I returned to most often other than Chekhov is *The Way of the Pilgrim*, by Mikhail Kozlov, since I still envision my son and me as wanderers exploring the Russian wilderness from village to village. But for us, those villages come in the form of train cars, and the villagers are our fellow passengers.

Fourteen

Tiger, Taiga

There is massive burning of the tundra and it has led to a cat-astrophic deluge. The conductor reports that the waters have risen more than twenty-four feet and are the worst in more than one hundred and twenty years. He received word it is already thought to be the costliest flood disaster in Russian history, and it is still growing. Apparently, the waters are almost covering the tracks ahead. We are too far south of the last major station and too far north of Vladivostok for there to be any place to eat or stay. This is wilderness—flooded wilderness, making it harder for wildlife to find food. Here we are, drinking tea and wondering if we are about to be forced off the train in the ti-ger-saturated taiga. At least that is how I envision it.

A fellow traveler reading the news tells me now that the river in this region has swollen to anywhere from five to twenty miles wide from its normally narrow reach. Others report of bears, displaced by the water, encroaching on villages, and now word comes of strong rainstorms moving down from the northwest.

Soldiers have been deployed, and in the rare areas of dry land, we pass military convoys where villagers have abandoned their fragile homes. The waters are not expected to fully recede until September, three weeks away. Even China, apparently, has evacuated tremendous swatches of territory along their side of the Amur a mere stone's throw away.

Word has come that some of the stone ballast supporting the tracks have been washed away, but no one in this car knows if it is in front of us or behind us or on an adjoining line. Everyone is converging either on the windows overlooking the river, or the dining car overlooking the vodka.

Trees are breaking like twigs. Someone saw cattle floating downstream.

Some settlements are being relocated with a military escort, as at least four dams have collapsed. No one yet knows about casualties, but one man said that on the best of days in the taiga it can be difficult. "I wouldn't be caught dead there," another quipped. Funny. It will not be good if we cannot get through. Worse if we have to leave the train.

We continue along the Amur River, China to the west, North Korea not far and Vladivostok to the south at the end of the line. At one point we passed an abandoned mission on the other side of the border. This 19th century sun-bleached structure sits in the woods near the river like the last building left in an old ghost town, made more obvious by the dark green hills and the deep green and swollen Amur. With the seaport of Vladivostok less than two days away, I thought our journey was almost over, but it seems we've run into a problem; not our first on the Siberian railroad, but certainly the most serious. There is talk of closing down the rails.

If this is true, we will be forced to disembark at one of the small stations nearby. I look out the window at the rising waters, suddenly uncertain of our whereabouts. "I wonder where we are," I say to no one in particular.

"Remember that book I was reading," Michael says. "*The Tiger,* by John Valliant?"

"I do. The one about the tiger that eats people."

"Yes, the non-fiction one."

"What about it?"

"That's where we are."

While few people wander this area of the wilderness where a tiger stalked people, ate them, and was finally caught (but, to be sure, there are other tigers somewhere outside), there was a time when some Russians freely emigrated here from the western cities. During World War One and throughout the Civil War which followed, western Russia was unstable with an ineffective Czar and revolution throughout the region from Moscow to St. Petersburg. With the growing opportunities in agriculture in the east, people packed up and headed to the small villages along the rails and around Lake Baikal. It is easy to wonder what would bring people so far from what can best be described as "the future" to live in a world so remote that most of its citizens had been sent here against their will, first to populate the area, and, if not, to die. At the time, an early death seemed likely; some from starvation, some from the cold and isolation, many from suicide. And not just a few poor souls were killed by wildlife, like the Amur tiger.

I look out the window a long time. I know we are not in danger from Tigers. As my father used to say, "They're more afraid of you then you are of them." Still, Dad was talking about cows. And I am not crazy about the coincidence of Michael reading about the feline massacre just before departing for Russia, but it is in my head, nonetheless. I whisper, more to myself than my son, "What immortal hand or eye dare frame thy fearful symmetry?"

Michael looks at me then back out the window. "They could be watching us now," he says. Punk.

John Valliant's book, *The Tiger*, records the story of the hunt for a tiger, or tigers, which completely devoured people, leaving shards of bones in its wake. Eventually, someone killed the suspected predator, and the stuffed cat is on display in a museum in Vladivostok. But this wilderness is home to upwards of five hundred Amur tigers, the largest of the Siberian tigers, often weighing over six hundred pounds.

The region is rich with other wildlife, including the sable fox and the Amur leopard. The Amur tiger had been endangered, but thanks to the efforts of conservationists—none of whom most likely ever faced being stranded out here—the Amur tiger is safe from extinction for now. It has eyesight five times better than humans and has been recognized as one of the most cautious, secretive, and dangerous animals in the forests. The grey wolf of the area, however, might be more of a threat due to its numbers. On top of being plentiful, they travel in large packs and, if threatened, one cry from the alpha wolf and they can easily devour a human. This is not common, however, unless their food is in short supply, which happens during floods.

Equally dangerous is the wild boar. The bears and wolves will generally avoid humans unless threatened, but the boar with bad eyesight and a small brain will simply charge. They weight about 400 pounds and will not be taken down by a single shot, assuming anyone has a gun to begin with, which is unlikely. If we do get stranded and can tolerate the woods to find food, it is the lynx that will be our demise. They live in the trees and attack from above while humans forage for mushrooms and berries. Yet it is what remains invisible to the eye that can essentially kill you. The tick is common in summer ready to dig deep into the skin and incite encephalitis. Also, the karakurt spider is one of the ten most deadly arachnids in the world. They are more common back in the Moscow region but they terrorize the taiga on summer nights, and their bite causes excruciating pain which spreads throughout the bitten limb, and then to the chest and the rest of the muscles.

But the tigers that eat people live in this area, and they probably had companions, so that is on my mind as we creep across trusses traversing rivers that even a newcomer like myself can clearly see are well beyond flood stage, and it will only get worse further south toward Vladivostok. Unfortunately, we had been reassured not to worry about mosquitoes carrying malaria as they only pester people along the southern borders and the region running toward the Sea of Japan when the region floods. No one could predict rising waters a month ahead of time. This is all just bad timing.

Chekhov said the Amur region was the most beautiful he had ever seen. In a letter to his brother, he insisted, "Do whatever you can to be exiled here!" He wrote of the vast landscape around us, which I must say is still as rugged and intimidating, and beautiful, as in his day. He wrote, "I am in love with the Amur, and would be happy to stay here for a couple of years. It is beautiful with vast open spaces and freedom, and it is warm. Switzerland and France have never known such freedom; the poorest exile breathes more freely on the Amur than the highest general in Moscow."

The juxtaposition is astonishing. This potentially life-threatening situation plays out beneath us in what is one of the lushest regions of Russia. It is odd to stare into the forest and simultaneously see such beauty and imminent danger. It is warm out and under bridge after bridge the river is well over her banks. Our cabin has a large window, but the hallway down the west side of the car has an almost aerial view of the rising waters. Local passengers from Vladivostok point to fallen trees and floating structures, talk to each other and gasp. I have spent my entire life on the coast and along rivers, but I've never seen so many submerged farms and roads, and even a few houses flooded to the rooftops.

I try to recall how my father kept his cool in situations like this, but then I realize he was good enough of a father to not get us into situations like this. I know fathers always question their decisions as dads. The truth is, maybe young fathers are merely understudies, even when our own children are two decades on, until our own father dies and we are forced into the role alone, no backup to call for advice or a calming voice. It is the true loss of security. I wonder if my father would have been a different dad had my grandfather lived beyond my fifth year. I am sure that I'm a better father now, despite placing my son in grave danger on the far side of the world, because my father remained in our lives for so long, offering me an example, a silent foundation upon which to stand. Well, we find ourselves here nonetheless, and I have learned to remain calm—not because I've mastered the art of keeping my cool but because I'm painfully aware, as all of us are in the halls of the carriages and the booths of the dining car, we can't do a damn thing about this except look out the window and wait. Fortunately, it is beautiful, this Amur region of Siberia.

South of here is the main bridge over the Amur, built in just over four years during World War One, and to be employed on the project was a privilege since people were paid significant amounts to get the job done. From the start it was called "The Amur Miracle," and is not only the largest bridge span of the trans-Siberian railway, it's the largest in the country. As we approach, people come out of their cabins to see the expanse of the water beneath the famous bridge. The hallway windows are lined with men, a few children, one woman. They do not talk much; they take pictures with their cellphones and just watch. From this height it is hard to see just how fast the water is running until a tree drifts by, or a shed door, the occasional sign. I grow more anxious; it feels like forever since we stood on the station platform buying food, safe from the possibility of abandoning the carriage in a remote area.

I wish we had known about the possibility of impassable tracks while at the last stop. The old women there who sold us dried fish and meat patties were fantastically friendly, and the passengers we met from the region remain among the kindest and most inquisitive. They are all fine traveling companions in spite of their silence as we all have a growing awareness of the potential tragedy outside. And the closer we get to Vladivostok, the less it feels like we will arrive anytime soon. As we move toward the end of the line, Michael wanders to take pictures of a once-in-a-century flood, and I head to the dining car to write it all down, but the tender here tells me they are out of vodka and beer. I drink water and while I wish to write, I cannot help but continue to watch outside.

"What the hammer? what the chain,
In what furnace was thy brain?
What the anvil? what dread grasp,
Dare its deadly terrors clasp!"

Fifteen

Fathers and Sons

It is late and we are almost there. I am in the dining car one last time and I am certain Michael is back in the cabin, asleep. He probably read some of the book he brought along, Walter Ciszek's *With God in Russia*, by the light of his small, black, pinpoint lamp attached to the binder of the book. But I could not sleep, so I've come back here one last time to write one more time.

Dear Michael,

Just months after you were born, I made my first trip to Russia. The Soviet Union had just died. Boris Yeltsin was the president, and his first duty was to keep the nation alive. Everyone in St. Petersburg and in Moscow was still trying to figure out what to do; after all, a new nation was born. It did not "return" to any previous, more glorified state; it had never known democracy. It had been a communist nation preceded by a czarist empire, and the powers that be were people not used to asking for help from anyone. Mistakes were common.

That was me when you came into this world, and like all new fathers I made decisions based on what I needed to do in order to keep you alive, then came the decisions based on what I remembered from growing up or from watching other young fathers. The hardest part of parenthood is knowing when to be there for you and when to back off. If I have mixed them up from time to time, forgive me.

Yet here we are at the end of one of the greatest journeys in modern travel. The irony is most fathers of twenty-year-old's only go to the train station to wave goodbye, not to embark on a month-long adventure. Maybe you would have rather done this alone; maybe with someone your own age. I am certain either of those is most likely preferable to traveling with your father, but we find ourselves here, nonetheless. Consider it your gift to me; my heart is full.

As I write this, I am looking out at the early morning light revealing itself over the Sea of Japan. At what point you will actually read this is a mystery to me since I'm not sure if I'll even mail it, and if I do it certainly won't be anytime soon. Between now and then, who is to say what will happen—to me, to you, to us. We have done okay together though; we understand each other and maybe that is all a father can ask for. It is probably well more than a son can ever expect.

So to abuse the metaphor of this journey just one more time—I do not know what's ahead or when we will split off at some point and follow different tracks. I am lucky we stayed on the same ride as long as we have. Thank you for that.

If our relationship has suffered at all, the scars are nearly unrecognizable, subtle, mysterious; I think we have come out of these two decades mostly unblemished. But some questions haunt all fathers: Should I have pushed you out on your own sooner? Should I have encouraged you toward different paths? Maybe I said too much, not enough, the wrong advice. The best we can hope for is we did the best we could. You have the same quiet, contemplative manner as your grandfather, the same kindness and patience. In that way he was with us in spirit.

We are not completely leaving Siberia; she will catch up to us later from time to time when we notice a rolling green landscape or buildings painted royal blue. She will tug at our memory when we drink tea or play chess. And maybe at some inconceivable time from now when you are well beyond my years and I'm long gone, you'll look back to this journey and remember how we laughed together, discovered so much of the world together. Maybe, someday, you will be sitting somewhere and someone—perhaps a grandson of your own or maybe just two strangers on a bench playing chess—will be talking about fathers and sons or sunsets on a summer night, and you'll think of me. If you do, I hope you will smile and remember the time when we were both so much younger and so very much alive, and we walked the hills near Lake Baikal. I hope you'll remember when we joined our Russian friends in the dining car for drinks and music, and time didn't pass us by as much as we left it behind.

And in the recesses of your mind there may be the faint echo of music. If so, I hope you will recall how we stood alone together between the cars where you played the harmonica and I watched the passing landscape of birch trees and green fields, just the two of us, enjoying this random trip through time.

Love,
Dad

Sixteen

Departures

We made it past the flooded plains and have arrived. I sit up early before departing the train for the city, then the airport, then home. My bags lay packed on the floor, the linens already rolled up and bagged for the attendant. Outside the sky is grey but clearing, and the morning sun picks up glints of glass on the skyscrapers of the city. Michael returns with his last cup of tea from the samovar and sits across from me on the opposite, now empty, bunk, our knees nearly knocking.

When the engine pulled us across the last sets of trusses and we saw the small, hilly skyline of Vladivostok, everyone breathed sighs of relief as the flooded Amur spared this train, though in our wake waits the inevitable submersion of these same tracks, disrupting the lives of travelers just a few days behind us.

The rare still-dry fields we passed heading south on this peninsula toward Vladivostok are clearly the land of laborers. Farmers and fisherman, lumberjacks and rail workers all jockey for position, try to make a living. The non-forest land is checkered with farms separated by fences made from trees, and small, lush gardens of cabbage sit inside makeshift fences, endless tiny plots each with its own tool shed. Cattle wander at will on all sides of the waterways, and fields of potatoes and onions stretch across the hills. I am sure it is an isolated life, but those we've met from this area do not imply loneliness.

The sweeping generalizations I have heard about Siberia, and Russia in general for that matter, have no support, no evidence of how such trite judgments might have started to begin with. Certainly, political propaganda fed the fears of all of us, but nothing here is the same as I had been taught. Nothing.

If I were to ride these rails again, I would spend more time on the platforms buying fry cakes, pirogies, dried fish, flat bread and fruit from the local women, and talk to them more, engage in what is clearly their existence, that walk from their home to the station and back.

In town too, the food is fine, from caviar crepes to real haggis, and delicious coffee at "coffee trucks" set up much like beer keg trucks at festivals back home. The connection I have discovered no matter where I travel, but in particular somewhere as remote as the rural sections of what is essentially already rural Siberia, is the food. It is the common denominator, and just like the chess games onboard brought us together with strangers, it is food which binds us—not language. I have been on trains throughout the United States, in particular the commuter routes from Manhattan to Long Island, and people who do share a language don't talk anyway, so this isn't much different. In fact, it has been far more engaging; too much common ground can kill a relationship.

Still, across this vast empire I believe the reason I spend so much time looking out at the wild landscape, the small royal-blue shacks and yellow station houses, the deep truth of birch trees, the small villages and eroding towns, is that they need no translation, no subtitles. I can let my imagination drone over the landscape without the need for inquiry or answer. Certainly, I would like to know the story behind an apparently abandoned gulag, or what the primary occupations are so far from any town of note, but that information is encyclopedic, and anyway, between cabinmates and dining car chess players, we seem to have discovered a decent cross-section of eastern Siberian culture. None of the people are rude; they are guarded. Their excited reaction to various topics is at first defensive, yet as soon as they discover our attempt to communicate and learn, they have patience and openly desire to engage and assist. This is all accompanied by frustration on both parts when we try too hard. The railway has taught me to not try so hard. This journey was worth every kopeck.

But there is a price to pay. A part of you dies with each new passage, and at some point, you understand there is no end of the line, there is only moving on, separately, praying the other is well, healthy, still moving forward. I have gone as far as I can on this wild trip with my son, and it is all so familiar from my own youth. I was twenty, my father fifty-five. He drove me to the airport for my one-way flight away from home toward something else with a vocabulary I had not yet even tried to translate. I just knew I needed to go, and he let me. It is my turn. That's our job, as parents, to let them go.

I can hear people disembarking, and I look at Michael and smile. He turns to me from looking out at the bright yellow, three-story buildings of Vladivostok's large trans-Siberian railway station and seems as restless as me.

"What?" he says, when I let out a small laugh.

"Springsteen."

He stares back out the window trying to dial up a train song by one of his favorites. Nothing. *Of course not*, I think. This one's for the fathers:

I will provide for you
And I'll stand by your side
You'll need a good companion
For this part of the ride
Leave behind your sorrows
Let this day be the last
Tomorrow there'll be sunshine
And all this darkness past
Big wheels roll through fields
Where sunlight streams
Meet me in a land of hope and dreams

Notes

The following are selected excerpts from the author's journals.

1. It's only day two but we are covering vast areas of wilderness with scatterings of cattle about. I can't get over the beauty. The pictures of Siberia I grew up with are of either snow or industrialization. But we are covering hundreds of miles so far with distant reaches of green pasture, birch trees, rolling hills of deep green and wildflowers everywhere, yellow and violet and red.

2. One of our cabinmates on this leg of the journey is a toss between Vladimir Putin and Liam Neeson. More Liam. He smiles a lot, checks his watch, and stares out the window like he's trying to decide whether or not to exit through it or use the door to his right. Meanwhile, there are two guys—twenty somethings—from Omsk in our carriage, and they have been hovering about us constantly, and I can't figure out if they want to practice their English or are scouting our belongings; really the only rude people of the trip so far. More often it feels uncomfortable. Late this afternoon one of them came in our cabin and despite my firm request that he leave, he pushed in further. Then Liam, without even looking up, said one word and the guy's face went white and he left quickly. Liam smiled at me and nodded, I said thank you, and he raised his cup of tea in a toast. We're on his good side.

3. It is much more difficult to write on a train than I thought it would be.

4. The random houses and, more-often, shacks out here seem to defy the landscape, particularly in winter, by being painted bright blue or stark yellow. There's nothing trite about Siberia in August.

5. It is startling when another train passes headed west. We can be moving along long enough, looking out the window, lost in the vast European landscape (for it remains Europe until we are in Yekaterinburg) as we barrel toward Asia, and my thoughts rise above the rumbling of our own car, so that the wilderness encompasses my being, and it can feel as if I am floating in silence, and I can almost hear the wind across the fields of wheat. Then a train rips through and our car shakes a bit, the noise broken every few seconds as the breaks between carriages on the other track create a vacuum of sorts in intervals. But then it is gone, and the quiet of our own train seems even more so, almost lonely, headed east toward emptiness.

6. Michael and I played chess for a while in the dining car, and a man, Dima, slightly drunk, well dressed, and polite with some English, asked if he could play. So Michael is doing that now while I'm in the next booth. I said to Dima, "I suppose everyone in Russia plays chess." And he told me that "only two types of people play chess in Russia: prisoners and crazy people." I asked which category he fell into, and he said, "I am in a category all my own." I laughed hard at his command of such a complicated reference in a language he clearly is not used to speaking. I like this guy. For now I'll assume he's in the latter group.

7. Michael's still playing chess, but I grew tired and came back

to stretch out on the bed, but our roommates have a movie blasting on a laptop. I've not read much about roommate etiquette while traveling in a cabin on a train, but surely, they can tell it is late, I'm tired, and it's loud. Still, I laughed as the Russian movie's soundtrack is by Louis Armstrong. I faded off to sleep somewhere between one small village and another listening to one of my favorite American Jazz musicians while Michael was two carriages away playing chess with some drunk Russian who might be either a prisoner or crazy. This is why I came. This is why we're here.

8. The train came to a screeching halt about three this morning. Michael and our mates here didn't wake, but I did; wide awake. We sat for an hour or so, and they never lowered the stairs to the platform, so we couldn't disembark. Both the cabin window and the one in the hallway looked out at dark woods and field, so there's no station here. I did read about the random cow meandering across the tracks at the wrong time, so it could easily be that, or some other animal. Still, it's a little disconcerting, particularly since the one movie we downloaded onto the laptop is Butch Cassidy and the Sundance Kid, and now I keep thinking of the train robbery scene.

9. One of the first questions people asked when I was planning this trip is about the cost. Well, I should probably write a chapter called "Economics" but I'm not sure I'd be able to tally it correctly. I know the tickets cost between 250 and 300 a person a leg for second class (four times one ticket to buy out the cabin and travel first class), and that included three meals per leg; that's three meals total. We chose dinner—rice with wood chips. The flights from NY to St Petersburg, roughly 700 per person, and a few hundred a piece for VISAS. In order to get the VISAS we need to prove we have a place to stay as well as the return tickets, so Igor

secured hotels in Petersburg, Yekaterinburg, Irkutsk, and Vladivostok, all ranging between sixty and one hundred a night, and then the not so cheap flights from Vladivostok back to St Petersburg, which is actually much further than flying from St Petersburg to New York. On board the train they only take rubles, no credit cards, and even then the bills must be small, they don't make change. So we had to carry a good amount of cash. ATM's are only available in the larger cities, and cash is needed as food isn't much cheaper than at home. This isn't an inexpensive venture. But now that I'm here, somewhere east of western Russia, and I just came in from standing on a station platform at three am under countless stars, cool air, nothing up north but the great forest, and Mongolia a chip shot to the south, and Michael is fast asleep in the cabin, and the air is so fresh I swear it's like drinking oxygen, I can't possibly calculate what it would have cost to not have come to begin with.

10. Next time I'll only buy food from the ladies at the stations whose lives revolve around the arrival time of the train, and they wander down the dirt path from their village to the platform and sell pastries, dried fish, pizza, pirogies, fresh fruit, and more, all less expensive than the least expensive grocer back home, and all fresh. I've been buying from them once we figured out a few stops into the trip. Alexander bought extra dried fish to share with us, and more tea, and gifts for his daughter and grandkids, and we sat a long time in silence eating, drinking, and watching the rain against the window in our cabin. One of those perfect moments.

11. Michael was coughing in the hallway, trying to shake his cold, when I heard a neighbor talk to him in Russian and with, apparently, hand signals. He gave Michael a jar of homemade Siberian honey to put in his tea, which he did, and he is doing so much better. This neighbor is now among

the "quicks" of our lives. That's what I've taken to calling those individuals who blow across our paths like a small dust devil, barely slowing down, for better or for worse, and move on leaving behind a significant memory, something to carry with us and pull out from time to time. This man was for the better; a good quick we call him. The cough is gone.

12. After two days of sweating our asses off in the cabin because the air won't come on, our new roomie Liam reached up above the window and switched something from left to right and it is suddenly much cooler. Go figure. I tried asking the carriage attendant about it, but I did so by waving my hand at my face like we do when we want to show how hot it is. She poured me a cup of tea.

13. One hundred years ago even the birches must have noticed the workers, new to this wilderness, taking breaks and eating blinis under their branches. Blinis bought by knocking on village doors and offering a few kopecks for food. The women must have handed them a tray of food for the pittance, not yet knowing what unfathomed future was about to steamroll into their lives. And the lakes and rivers, the swamps and marshes must have heard the iron beams beaten into the earth, the piles of steel, the cement and the plows, the workers speaking Russian, of course, but also Scottish, German, as horses pulled heavy saw-like beams of metal to cut a scar through this forest.

14. This is one massive mother of a country.

15. Travel by train is as annoying as it is exhilarating. It takes patience and flexibility; it takes a gregarious person who also happens to enjoy extended periods of absolute silence. Still, it is the only way to truly see and experience this remote and ancient empire save walking.

16. The great contrast for us is the juxtaposition from our life on the train to our life in the cities. In Yekaterinburg, we walked between fifteen and twenty miles a day to explore the riverfront, to wander through the Grunge Music Festival, and to explore the shops and pubs along the marketplace streets. Then we returned on board where for the next few days our longest stretch of the legs was the thirty feet to the dining car or the twelve feet to the passageway between cars.

17. I like to think that Jack Reed is on board, up front somewhere working on a speech. And Emma Goldman just returned to their cabin with tea to help him sooth is one remaining kidney, and they're arguing because she tells him that communism isn't working; that it is a great idea, but it simply can't work because of the basic corruption tendencies of humans. This pisses off Reed. Maybe Trotsky's with them trying to get as far away from Stalin as possible. He's going to train to Japan and catch a boat to the states and then head down to Mexico to hang with Kahlo and Rivera before he dies. I was about to bring Solzhenitsyn on board, but we're stopping. Again. This gives me a chance to walk out and look at the rolling stretches of trees, almost mystical in their presence. Oddly, many of the trees have no tops, as if they'd be cut off at the neck. Still, I don't see any debris. A storm perhaps, some time ago.

18. "So was I once a swinger of birches."

19. Irkutsk is a great town. It is obviously a city with skyscrapers and industry, but it has a small-town feel to it, and a strong young presence. It reminds me of Worcester, Massachusetts. I'm not sure what the next closest city might be, but it feels like we're really alone out here. I understand why this was a place for exiles and dissidents. The people here are all polite and pleasant. Still, we are deep into Russia now.

Yekaterinburg was still technically in Europe and has that western aura about it. But here in Irkutsk, it reminds me of Russia in the very early nineties just after the coup, when everything still had a tinge of Sovietness about it. The streets are named after Soviet leaders—Stalin, Lenin, and even Marx. The CCCP symbols remain emblazoned on buildings and there are more than a few monuments to Soviet leaders throughout the town.

20. This is a laborer's land. Farmers and fisherman; lumberjacks, jockeying for position, trying to make a living.

21. A Scene from Anywhere: We passed fields of tomato plants, and on the side of the tracks along a path was a young boy on a bike, waving to us, and next to him a small dog, his tail wagging. Is there a Russian Norman Rockwell? If so, he would have painted this moment, two people waving from the train, the dog, the boy, the tomatoes, the sky a dark blue. Humanity does have a center of gravity, after all.

22. Alexander Ivanovich is the first Russian in twenty years to ask me what I do for a living. When I tell him I am a professor, he seems impressed, and suddenly he wants to learn more English, share his vodka, his tea, and he comes to life again. He is drunk most of the time, but even then, he is friendly and remains the only passenger who has consistently and enthusiastically tried to constantly communicate with us. I ask his profession but he either doesn't understand or doesn't wish to answer. That's okay; I'll make up his story. It'll pass the long night.

23. This is not a trip to town to pick up groceries and go home, like we used to do when Michael was a toddler. This is a trip literally around the world, but it wasn't much more difficult to pull off; we made a list, figured out how much we'd need,

made sure we had the time, and we left. Perhaps the most significant lesson this trip has taught us is how easy it is to follow through on a wild idea.

24. Upon our return on board from a stop, none of the four of us could open our locked cabin door; neither could the attendant with a key. Another passenger who had a crowbar (this is how life is here; Russians carry random shit all the time), pried upon the door and we thanked him. Russia.

25. This is a stream of consciousness journey. Whatever happens triggers what happens next; and we rarely can live like that without ramifications; but here on the other side of the world, it is absolutely necessary to do so. Plus, we are here for the ramifications.

26. For a train ride during which the day can become quite predictable, nothing has been redundant or boring.

27. Alexander and I are teaching each other words. Rain: Dozhd. Bug: Oshibka. Rabbit: Krolik. We saw these out the window, and so we taught each other each other's languages. It was solely for the moment; such is life in transit. Neither of us will ever need to know, use, or recall those word again, but sitting there on our bunks, sharing tea and dried fish, it helped pass the time and bring us closer, though I'll never meet him again in my life. Ever.

28. Alex is packed and ready to disembark. He started gathering his things at six am, and it is now 9:30 and he is ready. Goat: Kozel. Hot: Goryachiy. Very Hot: Ochen Goryacho. We laughed.

29. Imet khoroshuyu zhizn. Have a good life.

30. I need to write a letter to Michael thanking him for joining me on this trip. It is truly a father's dream. We've had no

scars in our life, certainly nothing as deep and permanent as an iron scar, forever embedded in our psyche. No, just the opposite. And I must give my father a call, let him know we made it. I wish he could have been with us. Did he ever dream of seeing the Far East? I wonder sometimes, when he was a young boy walking through the streets of Brooklyn, what were his dreams? And my son here now, packing his things as we ready to disembark here at the Sea of Japan, when he is walking the paths along the Chesapeake Bay, what are his dreams?

31. Like all other journeys in my life, now that I've arrived, I'm keenly aware I didn't have a yearning to reach some destination; I just wanted to be on the ride. It is satisfying to have stood on that walking bridge while one of the French family took our picture in front of the Great Vladivostok Railway Station, but it is also slightly disappointing. I wish that I could have slowed the whole thing down.

Many thanks to the following who published, awarded, or acknowledged various versions of excerpts from this manuscript:

The Maine Review

Kestrel: A Journal of Literature and Art

A View from This Wilderness

Blue Planet Journal

Warfare Journal

Ilanot Review

Connotation Press

Olive Press

Foliate Oak Journal

World War Two History Magazine

Columbia Journal

Southern Humanities Review

Nowhere Magazine

Litterateur Magazine

Wanderlust Journal

All Nations Press

Silver Birch Press

Foreign Literary Journal

Adirondack Literary Review

The Alabama Literary Review

And special thanks to Jacki Lyden, Elizabeth Rosner, Jane Varley, and my companions at "Love Comes in at the Eye" writers' workshop in Renvyle, Ireland, for their comments and tolerance. Also to my publisher, Kim Davis, and to my dear friend in Russia, Igor Chertok, whose assistance made the entire trip possible.

About the Author

BOB KUNZINGER is the author of nine collections of essays, including *A Third Place: Notes in Nature,* and *Penance: Walking with the Infant.* He lives in Virginia.

About the Photographer

MICHAEL KUNZINGER'S photography has appeared in publications such as *Kestrel*, *Blue Planet Journal*, and *St Anthony Messenger*, and has been in solo and group shows in Virginia, New York, and Galway, Ireland. His abstract work was featured for a solo exhibition at the renowned Quick Center for the Arts in New York, a finalist in an International Competition featured at The Louvre in Paris, and he is the author of the photo essay book, *Across The Wild Land: A Photographic Journey on the Trans-Siberian Railroad* from Blurb Books.

CPSIA information can be obtained
at www.ICGtesting.com
Printed in the USA
BVHW042003190522
637564BV00006B/76